Lincoln, Life-Size

Lincoln, Life-Size

By

Philip B. Kunhardt III

Peter W. Kunhardt

Peter W. Kunhardt, Jr.

Foreword by

Harold Holzer

Alfred A. Knopf, New York, 2009

THIS IS A BORZOI BOOK
PUBLISHED BY ALFRED A. KNOPF

Copyright © 2009 by Philip B. Kunhardt III, Peter W. Kunhardt,
and Peter W. Kunhardt, Jr.

www.aaknopf.com

Knopf, Borzoi Books, and the colophon are registered
trademarks of Random House, Inc.

Library of Congress Cataloging-in-Publication Data
Kunhardt, Philip B.
Lincoln, life-size / by Philip B. Kunhardt III, Peter W. Kunhardt,
and Peter W. Kunhardt, Jr.
p.   cm.
ISBN 978-0-307-27081-8
1. Lincoln, Abraham, 1809–1865—Pictorial works.
2. Lincoln, Abraham, 1809–1865—Portraits.   3. Presidents—
United States—Pictorial works.   I. Kunhardt, Peter W.
II. Kunhardt, Peter W., 1982–   III. Title.
E457.6.K857 2009
973.7092—dc22   2009020007

Manufactured in China

First Edition

Contents

Foreword

Lincoln, His Photographs, and Their Scholars

By Harold Holzer

"I cannot see why all you artists want a likeness of me," Abraham Lincoln once teased Peoria photographer Roderick M. Cole, "unless it is because I am the homeliest man in the State of Illinois." As usual when it came to Lincoln's self-deprecating remarks, there was a bit of truth in it, and a dose of hokum as well.

Lincoln knew precisely why camera artists—and, later, when their pictures could be widely reproduced, the general public—sought his likenesses. It was because he was famous, and one way that admirers could celebrate him was to preserve and display his pictures. The way photographers could profit from such demand was by reproducing and selling them. There is not much doubt why Lincoln accepted most invitations to pose, homeliness notwithstanding. He craved political success and sensed early on that photographs, especially retouched ones, could help earn him new admirers, particularly among those who had heard he was simply too ugly to qualify for high office.

Hence, as this definitive new book makes clear, the modest man who enjoyed joking about his unconventional appearance also made certain that he sat before the cameras more often than just about any of his contemporaries. That the results benefited him is beyond doubt. When he arrived in Washington for his inauguration in 1861, following a journey that ended in embarrassment—with a nocturnal flight through hostile Baltimore—the first two places the President-elect went to rebuild his faltering image were a church and Mathew Brady's photography studio. At the latter, he admitted to onlookers that Brady's imposing pre-election photograph (as much as his sensational Cooper Union address that same day) had "made me President."

It took decades for historians to catch up with Lincoln's remarkably early appreciation for the pictorial media. And it required one enlightened collector to save the endangered archive of photographic portraits, some of which had already perished in catastrophes like the Chicago Fire. As the nineteenth century ended, scholarship on the subject remained scant. For the most part, books had yet failed to reproduce photographs even as illustrations; when employed at all, Lincoln photos were merely engraved for frontispieces. But taste was changing. When *McClure's* magazine published the earliest photograph of Lincoln for the first time in 1895, the picture proved so appealing that even future president Woodrow Wilson wrote to say he would "treasure it."

Two years later a New York City businessman named Frederick Hill Meserve, born the year the Civil War ended, found himself in the right place at just the right time. The story goes that in 1897 he strolled into a Fifth Avenue auction house where, for reasons even he could not explain, he purchased for $1.10, sight unseen, a parcel of old photographic prints—including, as it turned out, precious images by Mathew Brady, who had died just a year earlier. Bitten by the collecting bug, Meserve by 1902 had acquired more than ten thousand of Brady's glass negatives, among them his signature Lincolns, and had launched a serious effort to catalog them systematically. Nine years later, in 1911, he issued his groundbreaking limited edition volume of 100 chronologically arranged Lincoln photographs, each painstakingly identified with an M (for Meserve) number for future reference. The album was so exquisitely produced—with each of its illustrations tipped in by hand—that the volume itself became a precious Lincoln collectible. Later amended with four supplements of eight photographs each in 1917, 1937, 1950, and 1955, it remained for thirty years the definitive account of Lincoln's photographs. In 1944 Meserve significantly widened its influence by publishing a popular edition entitled *The Photographs of Abraham Lincoln*, featuring an introductory essay by his friend Carl Sandburg. In this, his final chronological account, Meserve affirmed the number he had originally proposed three decades earlier: 100 known Lincoln pictures.

Three years before that book came off the press, however, a new voice was heard in the field. It was that of Stefan Lorant, a Hungarian-born editor who had become incurably enthralled by America's sixteenth President after reading his speeches while imprisoned in Hitler's Germany in the 1930s, before he gained his freedom and fled to England. Early in his career, Lorant helped invent the pictorial magazine format later popularized in the United States by *Life* and *Look*. He turned his full attention to Lincoln after he emigrated here just before America entered World War II. At first planning an illustrated biography designed like a picture magazine, Lorant found himself so intrigued by the illustrations he was gathering that he sought out Meserve and corresponded with experts like Herbert Wells Fay of Springfield and Louis A. Warren of the Lincoln National Life Foundation in Fort Wayne. "I soon discovered," Lorant recalled, "that the findings of different scholars were utterly contradictory. Month after month of research was spent in straightening out the discrepancies." Lorant elected to add an appendix to his little book, offering 92 photographic portraits accompanied by nine "scenes" taken outdoors, all arranged under a fresh numbering scheme. The total that Lorant proposed stood at 101, though the writer was certain additional pictures would come to light. He even included blank boxes in his chronology labeled "Space for *your* Lincoln photograph," urging: "If you have

a portrait of Lincoln which is not included in this pictorial bibliography, will you paste it in this space and notify the author of this book . . . so that he may include *your* portrait in a future edition." (That the process of affixing such antiques to the pages of his book might ruin them, or at least drastically reduce their monetary value, seems never to have occurred to him.)

It would not be quite as easy as Lorant hoped to find new and unknown Lincoln photos, but he persevered for almost thirty years more with some success. In 1952 he expanded and refined his original study into an illustrated biography entitled *Lincoln: A Picture Story of His Life*. "I have unearthed a number of pictures never known before," he boasted at the time. Among them was a recently discovered (though by someone else) image of Lincoln lying in state in his coffin in New York. Lorant's next revision appeared in 1957—it was the first Lincoln book this writer ever owned—and included a recently unearthed photograph of Lincoln waiting his turn to speak at Gettysburg. The author brought out yet another revised and enlarged edition in 1969, featuring 103 L-numbered prints, and with that, he wrote, "my research on Lincoln photographs, a task which I began twenty-eight years ago, comes to an end."

By then Lorant was facing stiff new competition in the field. In 1963 Dayton artist/collector Lloyd Ostendorf had joined forces with New York auction gallery impresario Charles Hamilton to produce a new book devoted exclusively to the camera portraits of the Civil War President: *Lincoln in Photographs: An Album of Every Known Pose*. "The pioneer works of Meserve are now out of date," the authors insisted in their preface, "and the pictorial biography of Lorant goes far afield from photography and does not include the most recent discoveries." The Hamilton-Ostendorf collection featured six previously unknown poses as well as others "reproduced for the first time from the original glass negative or collodion plates, unretouched and uncropped." Ostendorf contributed a highly useful effort to show twin-image stereo cards as they once looked, side by side, on their original cardboard mounts and, with rather less interest, to reassemble the multiple (and only microscopically different) variants taken by four-lens cameras to speed the printing of *carte de visite*–sized prints for public sale. Now identified with O numbers, the Ostendorf total reached 118.

For the next six or seven years, before Lorant moved on to new areas of interest, these two historians jockeyed (and occasionally battled) over Lincoln photographs. Ostendorf gleefully pointed out Lorant's misunderstanding of technical issues like multiple-lens photography, and Lorant retaliated against Ostendorf and his collaborator, accusing them of "naiveté and ignorance" and suggesting their book was a "hodgepodge of undigested data, misleading information, and wild guesses."

The rivalry came to a head with the discovery in 1969 of an unknown Lincoln portrait by Alexander Gardner, taken in August 1863. For nearly a century it had escaped notice, buried in the papers of Lincoln's onetime secretary John Hay. When Ostendorf arranged with Hay's descendants to introduce it in the journal *Lincoln Herald*, Lorant trumped him by publishing the picture in *Life*. In truth, neither man had actually found the picture, merely earned equal privilege to announce its discovery. But their feud only got hotter, with Ostendorf insisting that the Hay family had not granted permission to reprint the picture "in any commercial magazine." Understandably, when James Mellon II published *The Face of Lincoln* in 1979, easily the most handsome and lavish album of photographs issued to date, he prudently avoided making the project a new catalogue raisonné and diplomatically refused to take sides between the warring historians.

Ostendorf, far younger than his rival, ultimately enjoyed the last word—that is, until now. In 1985 he brought out an updated and enlarged edition of his venture with Hamilton, its last two pages featuring seven hitherto unknown photographs, some of them variants of previously recorded images and others distant scenes of Lincoln's first inaugural. But here too was one spectacular new image of Lincoln seated on the Capitol portico on March 4, 1865, awaiting his second swearing-in, his hair and beard so closely trimmed he was all but unrecognizable save for his huge ears and long legs. The historian now counted 126 Lincoln photos in all.

And he was not yet done with the subject. Conceding the following decade that Lincoln photographs had become "increasingly hard to find," he nonetheless argued in 1998 that "new finds and new data make an up-to-date numbering of photographs essential" and that year published an amended and retitled version of his thirty-five-year-old original, which inexplicably dropped Hamilton's name as coauthor. *Lincoln's Photographs: A Complete Album* took the numbering sequence to 130 but aroused significant controversy with its latest "discoveries," including a fuzzy picture of a bearded, top-hatted man on the deck of a boat and an admittedly "obscure . . . long shot" purportedly showing "a distant silhouette of President Lincoln" standing in front of the White House.

Most sensational of all was a postmortem profile, which, Ostendorf argued, showed the murdered President the day after his death. Though the photo boasted a strong provenance—it had belonged to artist John B. Bachelder, who later collaborated on a painting and engraving of Lincoln's dying moments—most experts dismissed it as a blatant fake. The supposed corpse's hair looked much too perfectly coiffed, and its features seemed suspiciously unmarred by the horrors of his death struggle. It seemed far more likely to some that Bachelder had simply made a realistic-looking sketch of Lincoln as a model for the deathbed picture, then photographed the result for easy reference. But Ostendorf never retreated from his claim.

"These cameras," Lincoln had once remarked during a visit to the Brady galleries, "are painfully truthful." By the dawn of the twenty-first century, however, it had become all too apparent that none of the existing compilations of Lincoln photographs could quite make the same assertion. And although Stefan Lorant, for one, declared in 1969 that he doubted "any more genuine Lincoln photographs could come to light," the search that Frederick Hill Meserve began before the twentieth century continued in earnest into the twenty-first, fueled by frequent rumors of fresh new discoveries, while the yearning for a definitive chronology only grew.

This new book was much needed and long overdue. And in a happy coincidence that neatly completes a circle of devoted scholarship after more than a century of effort, this latest and most authoritative edition has been produced by the descendants of the very man who single-handedly invented the Lincoln photograph field. As the subject of all these pictures—the man who supposedly did not like to have his picture taken but somehow did so, more than 110 times—might well have observed: it is "altogether fitting and proper."

Throughout the first half of the twentieth century Frederick Hill Meserve cataloged Lincoln portraits, mounting four per page in workbooks that he updated as he discovered new images.

Photographs of Lincoln in 1858
from The MESERVE Collection   148 East 78 St
New York

MESERVE No. 7
Beardstown, Ill.
May 7, 1858
by Abraham B. Byers

MESERVE No. 3
Chicago, Ill.
July 10, 1858
by P. von Schneider

MESERVE No. 10
Macomb, Ills
Aug. 26, 1858
by W. P. Pearson

MESERVE No. 11
Macomb, Ills.
Aug. 28, 1858
by W. P. Pearson

Lincoln's Face

Philip B. Kunhardt III

Lincoln's face is the most recognizable in American history—a face that today evokes widespread respect and even reverence. But through most of his life, Lincoln's face mostly inspired laughter, and a widespread opinion that he was incredibly homely. From every phase of his life people offered the same opinion. Childhood acquaintance H. E. Dummer called him "an uncouth looking lad." Elliott B. Herndon of Springfield described him as a "sort of monstrosity"—with a huge muscular body, a disproportionately small head, and a "lascivious mouth," making him an unattractive "cross between Venus and Hercules." "He was not a pretty man by any means," agreed his brother William Herndon, Lincoln's law partner for nearly seventeen years. He had "dark," "shriveled," and "leathery" skin and overall looked "woe struck." Journalist Donn Piatt said he was "the homeliest man I ever saw," his face appearing "dull, heavy, and repellent." Charles Barry, who painted Lincoln in 1860, recalled the "long, wiry neck," "the uncombed hair," "the cavernous sockets beneath the high forehead," and the "busy eyebrows hanging like curtains" over his eyes. Fellow Republican Isaac Arnold described Lincoln as "rough" and "grotesque"; and Union officer Theodore Lyman deemed him simply "the ugliest man I ever put my eyes on."

From the testimony of those who knew him came a vivid description of Lincoln's appearance. All agreed his face was long and angular and, as eleven-year-old Grace Bedell wrote, extremely thin. He had large ears, and what was described as a "prodigious" mouth, which he pursed, Mary Lincoln reported, when he became decisive on any subject. His nose was distinctive—"a prominent organ," wrote British journalist William Howard Russell, that "stands out from the face, with an inquiring, anxious air, as though it were sniffing for some good thing in the wind."

Lincoln's eyes were what people most remembered, but descriptions of them often conflicted. Some said they were "bluish brown," others "grey," and others "hazel." William Russell called them "dark," "deeply set," and "penetrating," but also "full of an expression which almost amounts to tenderness." Many recalled how Lincoln rarely combed his hair, adding to a general unkempt appearance. They described his ill-fitting suits and worn-out boots, pulled on as often as not over dirty old socks. To many, Lincoln's skin had a sallow, unhealthy look; some claimed that his body gave off odors due to poor digestion.

Lincoln took all the criticism with good humor and liked to joke about himself. He was once out splitting rails, he told a friend, when a man walked by with a gun and aimed it at him. When asked what he was doing, "the man replied that he had promised to shoot the first man he met who was uglier than himself." After examining the man's face, Lincoln tore open his shirt and replied, "If I am uglier than you, then blaze away." (The artist Francis Carpenter, who painted Lincoln in 1864, told a different version of this story that he said he heard directly from the President. In early adulthood Lincoln was once "accosted . . . by a stranger, who said,

'Excuse me, sir, but I have an article in my possession which belongs to you.' He then presented Lincoln with a jack-knife. 'This knife,' said he, 'was placed in my hands some years ago, with the injunction that I was to keep it until I found a man uglier than myself. . . . Allow me to say, sir, that I think you are fairly entitled to the property.' ") When Stephen A. Douglas, in the famous debates, called his opponent two-faced, Lincoln is said to have answered, "I leave it to my audience. If I had another face, do you think I'd wear this one?"

The stories went on and on. In Springfield when Lincoln was once offered a mirror so he could groom himself for a photograph, he said that "it would not be much of a likeness if I fixed up any." "Just look natural," a cameraman once said to him. "That is what I would like to avoid," he replied. And then later to friends that same day: "That cameraman seemed anxious about the picture, but, boys, I didn't know what might happen to the camera." Sending a portrait to his niece in 1858, he wrote, "This is not a very good looking picture, but it's the best that could be produced from the poor subject."

All this self-deprecating humor was offset by the fact that Lincoln was not ugly at all. When he was relaxed and quiet, his face was indeed unremarkable, possessing "no more expression than a post," recalled journalist Horace White. But "when enlivened in conversation or engaged in telling, or hearing some mirth-inspiring story," wrote his friend Robert Wilson, "his countenance would brighten up" and everything would begin to change. It did so almost in slow motion, Wilson recalled—first the face muscles would begin to contract, then "several wrinkles would diverge from the inner corner of his eyes, and extend down diagonally across his nose," then his eyes would begin to sparkle, and finally he would break out in a great unrestrained laugh. And here was the secret of Lincoln's chameleonlike appearance, recognized especially by artists. When Alban Jasper Conant arrived in Springfield, Illinois, in the summer of 1860 to paint Lincoln, he was first struck by "the deep, repellant lines of his face," which gave it an expression "easily mistaken for coarseness." But as the two men talked, the artist began to see an entirely different countenance, "and I admitted to myself that his frequent smile was peculiarly attractive." If in repose his face was heavy, agreed Donn Piatt, "it brightened like a lit lantern when animated. His dull eyes would fairly sparkle with fun, or express as kindly a look as I ever saw, when moved by some matter of human interest." William Herndon summed it up best in a lecture he gave on Lincoln in 1865: "When that eye and face and every feature were lit up by the inward soul or fire of emotion, *then* it was that all those apparently ugly features sprang to organs of beauty."

***

Lincoln was photographed more often than anyone before him—far more than Daniel Webster or Henry Clay, the two most photographed men of their times. As the ease of printing from

negatives transformed the field, and newspapers began to be able to run low-cost engravings from prints, the value of political portraiture expanded and Lincoln was its first great beneficiary. He also seems to have genuinely enjoyed the process; the hour or so spent at a photographer's studio he found relaxing, a good way to escape from his harrowing schedule. Though sometimes photographers came to him and set up makeshift studios, more often, at the urging of a friend or an artist who needed an image to work from, Lincoln went to them.

Of the 114 portraits of Lincoln, all but four were taken within a period of just seven years. They show him in a variety of attitudes. There is the "tousled hair" photo taken by Alexander Hesler in Chicago, in which Lincoln's "thatch of wild, Republican hair," as William Russell later described it, makes him look as if he has just awakened from a nap. There are pictures of Lincoln in dirty white suits; wearing oversize bow ties; and sporting various stages of facial hair (but never a mustache). In some pictures he looks like a riverboat gambler; in others he appears bashful, or haggard, or mule-faced, or goofy. In the thirty-nine beardless portraits taken before 1861 he varies from looking relaxed and confident, to exhausted and dreamy, to slightly depressed or faintly amused.

Exposure times were long in the 1850s—as much as a minute—during which time it was essential for the poser to remain still. This lent a rigidity to most of the portraits that led many of his friends to say they looked little like him, in life. As Lincoln's secretary and biographer John G. Nicolay clearly recognized, it was Lincoln's ever-changing expressions that communicated the face people remembered. "Graphic art," Nicolay recalled in the 1870s, "was powerless before a face that moved through a thousand delicate gradations of line and contour, light and shade, sparkle of the eye and curve of the lip, in the long gamut of expression from grave to gay, and back again from the rollicking jollity of laughter to that serious, far-away look that with prophetic intuitions beheld the awful panorama of war, and heard the cry of oppression and suffering. There are many pictures of Lincoln; there is no portrait of him."

The vast majority of Lincoln's photographs show him seated in a studio chair. Only twenty depict him standing—fourteen times outdoors in a group and six in a studio or indoors. Those full-length studio poses required a careful setup and special concentration on the part of the poser. Lincoln was photographed a few times in profile, documenting both left and right sides of his face.

In the best of the photographs, especially when he looked straight into the camera, there is a powerful sense of presence and of brooding intelligence. When a photograph was taken near the time of a pivotal event—just days before the Gettysburg Address, or shortly before the second inaugural—it could capture an almost spiritual quality.

In some of the pictures one of Lincoln's eyes looks half-asleep while the other stares wide-open. Cover half the face and each side looks like it belongs to a different person, one appearing downcast and uncertain, the other determined. This imbalance grew more pronounced when Lincoln was overtired. In some of the portraits his left eye has drifted upward, leaving more white underneath it than on the right. This upward creeping, which modern authorities have called "strabismus," grew more extreme during the presidential years, and by the time of the Gettysburg Address his eye had become partly obscured by the upper lid. Lincoln's left cheekbone also became increasingly pronounced over the years, further throwing off the symmetry of his face. And the right side of his mouth was usually turned downward while the left side turned up. A person speaking with him would in a sense face two Lincolns, one fiercely alert, the other soft and exhausted. By the time of his last months in office, one side of Lincoln's face looked his age, fifty-six, while the other looked like it could be eighty.

***

The text of this book is based on primary sources that we have chosen to shed light on Lincoln's state of mind at the time of each sitting. We have drawn them from Lincoln's own words, as well as from diary accounts, reminiscences, and letters from others. (The sources are all listed at the end of the book.) As coauthors we continue in the tradition of our forebears, Frederick Hill Meserve, Dorothy Meserve Kunhardt, and Philip B. Kunhardt, Jr. Each of them, as we are, was entranced by the face of Abraham Lincoln. In 1944 Meserve teamed up with Carl Sandburg and published *The Photographs of Abraham Lincoln.* "Artists and sculptors . . . have spoken of the fascination and the profound involvements to be seen in the face and physical form of Abraham Lincoln," Sandburg wrote. "The exterior man moved with some of the mystery of the interior man." Sandburg described Meserve as "the Zealot"—the man "best known for unquenchable interest in Lincoln photographs. . . . Quiet, modest, and unassuming, openly free-handed with friends and ungrudgingly generous with strangers, Meserve might be termed a 'born natural' in his portrait field." Two decades later Meserve's daughter, Dorothy Kunhardt, with her son wrote *Twenty Days,* the definitive pictorial treatment of Lincoln's assassination, that included an analysis of his face as seen through photographs. Commenting on an 1858 portrait, she wrote, "The picture plainly shows the seams and wrinkles that were evident in Lincoln's face even as a young man—as well as the deeply serious, almost sad expression of his eyes whenever he was photographed." Philip B. Kunhardt, Jr., carried on the family's fascination with the subject. He once wrote, "Lincoln's features were not normally treated kindly during his lifetime. . . . His ears were as big as flap-jacks, his nose like a beak, his skin was yellowed leather, his lower lip protruded. . . . Those who read behind the immediate features included many poets, artists, and writers. 'His eyes had an inexpressible sadness,' wrote the artist

Thomas Hicks, 'with a far-away look, as if they were searching for something they had seen long, long years ago.' "

This is a book about the personal Lincoln—about how his character was expressed in his face and in his words. Lincoln cared about people's faces and how they used them. Once, when a man came to see him in the White House and refused to look him in the eye, Lincoln became annoyed. "What's the matter with you?" he finally blurted out. "You can't look me in the face!" Faces mattered to Lincoln, and he believed he could judge character in them. Jokes about ugliness aside, he believed that the face was the window into a person's soul.

Just months after Lincoln's death, William Herndon interviewed Benjamin F. Irwin of Springfield. In 1860 Irwin had visited Lincoln at his home, bringing with him a local Democrat who wished to meet the Republican candidate. After a period Lincoln came downstairs to greet them, dressed in his shirtsleeves and "sock feet." He would later become famous for this—appearing at the door of the White House in a pair of old slippers, or agreeing to meet with his generals at night wearing only his nightshirt. Though inclined not to like him, Lincoln's guest left "bewitched." "I am an office holder under Buchanan," he told Irwin, "but I intend to vote for that man." "I have been told he was a fool & an ugly man," he said. "He's a man . . . of great good sense—familiar & honest. He's not an ugly man."

Over time the young man with odd features grew into a statesman whose inner qualities became visible—his tenacity and his compassion; his patience and his moral passion; his sensitivity and his stubbornness. Lincoln's face took on the story of his times. The Civil War became reflected in it, and the coming end of slavery. It is a face that still matters to us all these years later—the backwoods toughness still visible but transmuted by time and fate into a face of a refined sensibleness—a sane face, an earnest face, a wise face, a human face.

Lincoln, Life-Size

Probably **1846,** *Springfield, Illinois*

AL.c1846.1

Photograph by Nicholas H. Shepherd

In 1895 the journalist Ida Tarbell paid a visit to the home of Robert T. Lincoln in search of information about his father. He showed her this previously unpublished portrait, the earliest ever taken. Appearing in McClure's *magazine later that year, the picture caused a stir, showing Lincoln as a "man in the making," as one reader put it. Lincoln's old friend Henry C. Whitney wrote the following letter to the editor:*

My Dear Sir: I am greatly obliged for your early picture of Abraham Lincoln, which I regard as an important contribution to history. It is without doubt authentic and accurate; and dispels the illusion so common (but never shared by me) that Mr. Lincoln was an ugly-looking man. In point of fact, Mr. Lincoln was always a noble-looking—always a highly intellectual looking man—not handsome, but no one of any force ever thought of that. . . . This picture was a surprise and pleasure to me. I doubt not it is its first appearance. It will be hailed with pleasure by friends of Mr. Lincoln. . . . I never saw him with his hair combed before.

Probably **October 27, 1854,** *Chicago, Illinois*

AL.1854.1

Photograph by J.C.F. Polycarpus von Schneidau

After delivering a speech in Chicago in which he denounced the spread of slavery, Lincoln dined with George Schneider, the former editor of the Staat Zeitung, *an antislavery German-language newspaper. He then posed for this photograph. Lincoln's speech that day was never transcribed, but the* Chicago Journal *reported on the event.*

His speech of last evening was as thorough an exposition of the Nebraska iniquity as has ever been made, and his eloquence greatly impressed all hearers. . . . The impression created by Mr. Lincoln on all men, of all parties, was first, that he was an honest man, and, second, that he was a powerful speaker.

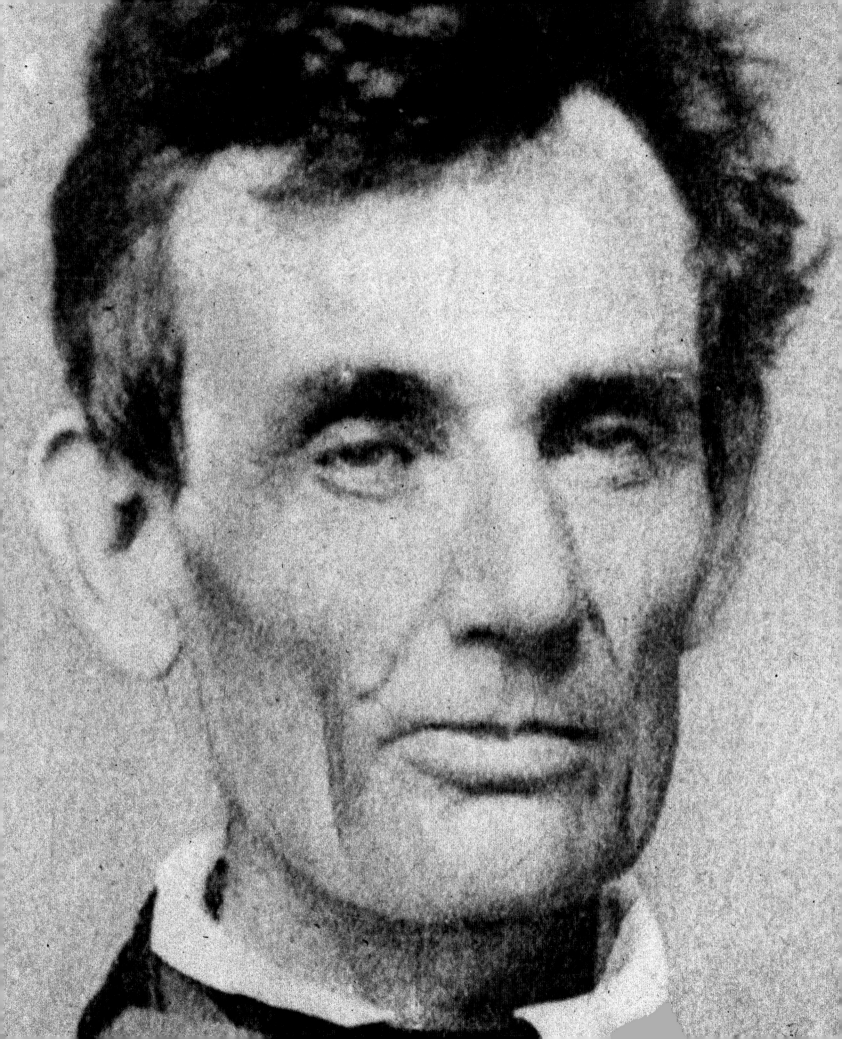

February 28, 1857, *Chicago, Illinois*

AL.1857.1

Photograph by Alexander Hesler

In the winter of 1857, before his nomination to the Senate, Lincoln was photographed at the Chicago studio of Alexander Hesler, who first tried to smooth down his hair. Not liking the results, Lincoln ran his fingers through it and messed it up but omitted mentioning this when he later told the story.

A short time before my nomination I was in Chicago attending a law-suit. A photographer of that city asked me to sit for a picture, and I did so. This coarse, rough hair of mine was in a particularly bad tousle at the time, and the picture presented me in all its fright. After my nomination, this being about the only picture of me there was, copies were struck to show those who had never seen me how I looked. The newsboys carried them around to sell, and had for their cry: "Here's your Old Abe, he'll look better when he gets his hair combed."

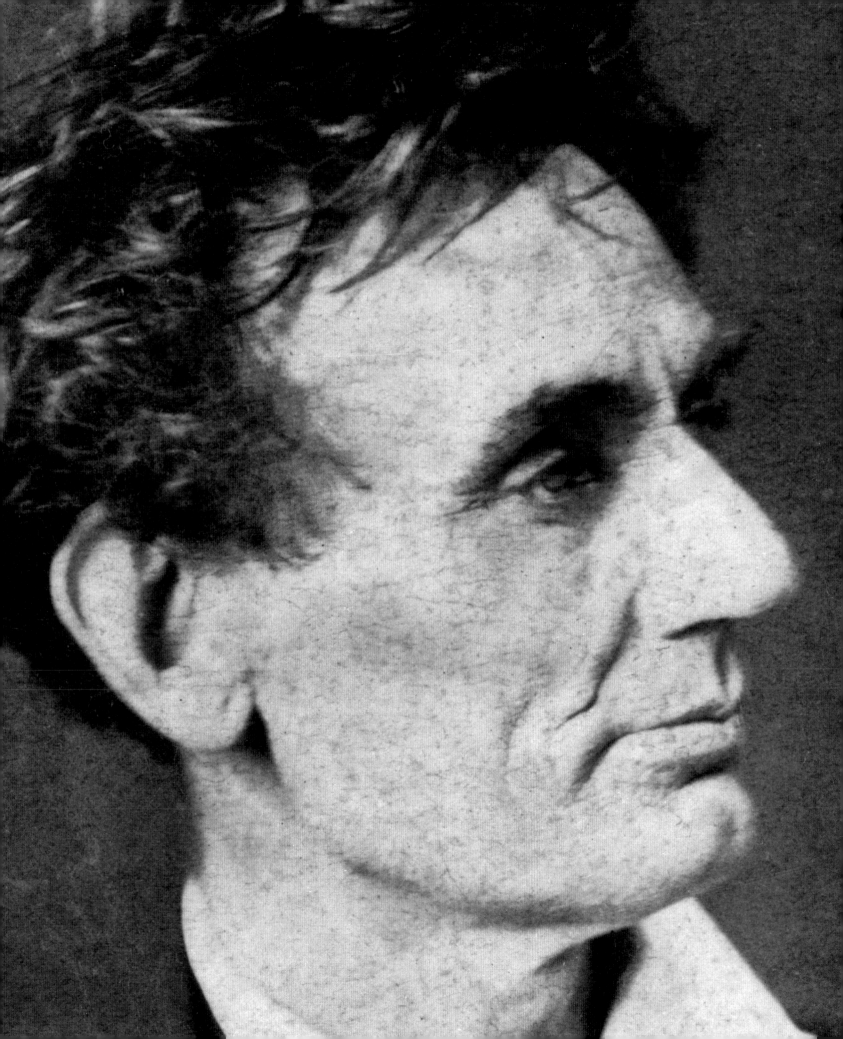

Possibly **May 27, 1857,** *Danville, Illinois*

AL.1857.2

Photograph by Amon J. T. Joslin

Just weeks after sitting for this portrait, Lincoln gave a speech in response to the Dred Scott decision, which had denied citizenship to all blacks in America. He contrasted the dismal new situation to the early days of the Republic.

In those days, our Declaration of Independence was held sacred by all, and thought to include all; but now, to aid in making the bondage of the negro universal and eternal, it is assailed, and sneered at, and construed, and hawked at, and torn, till, if its framers could rise from their graves, they could not at all recognize it.

April 25, 1858, *Urbana, Illinois*

AL.1858.1

Photograph by Samuel G. Alschuler

Twenty-three-year-old Joseph Oscar Cunningham, who regularly traveled the Eighth Circuit with Lincoln, was with him when this picture was taken, and later wrote about the sitting.

One morning I was in the gallery of Mr. Alschuler, when Mr. Lincoln came into the room and said he had been informed that he (Alschuler) wished him to sit for a picture. Alschuler said . . . he could not take the picture in that coat (referring to a linen duster in which Mr. Lincoln was clad), and asked if he had not a dark coat in which he could sit. Mr. Lincoln said he had not; that this was the only coat he had brought with him from his home. Alschuler said he could wear his coat, and gave it to Mr. Lincoln, who pulled off the duster and put on the artist's coat. Alschuler was a very short man, with short arms, but with a body nearly as large as the body of Mr. Lincoln. The arms of the latter extended through the sleeves of the coat of Alschuler a quarter of a yard, making him quite ludicrous, at which he (Lincoln) laughed immoderately, and sat down for the picture to be taken with an effort at being sober enough for the occasion. The lips in the picture show this.

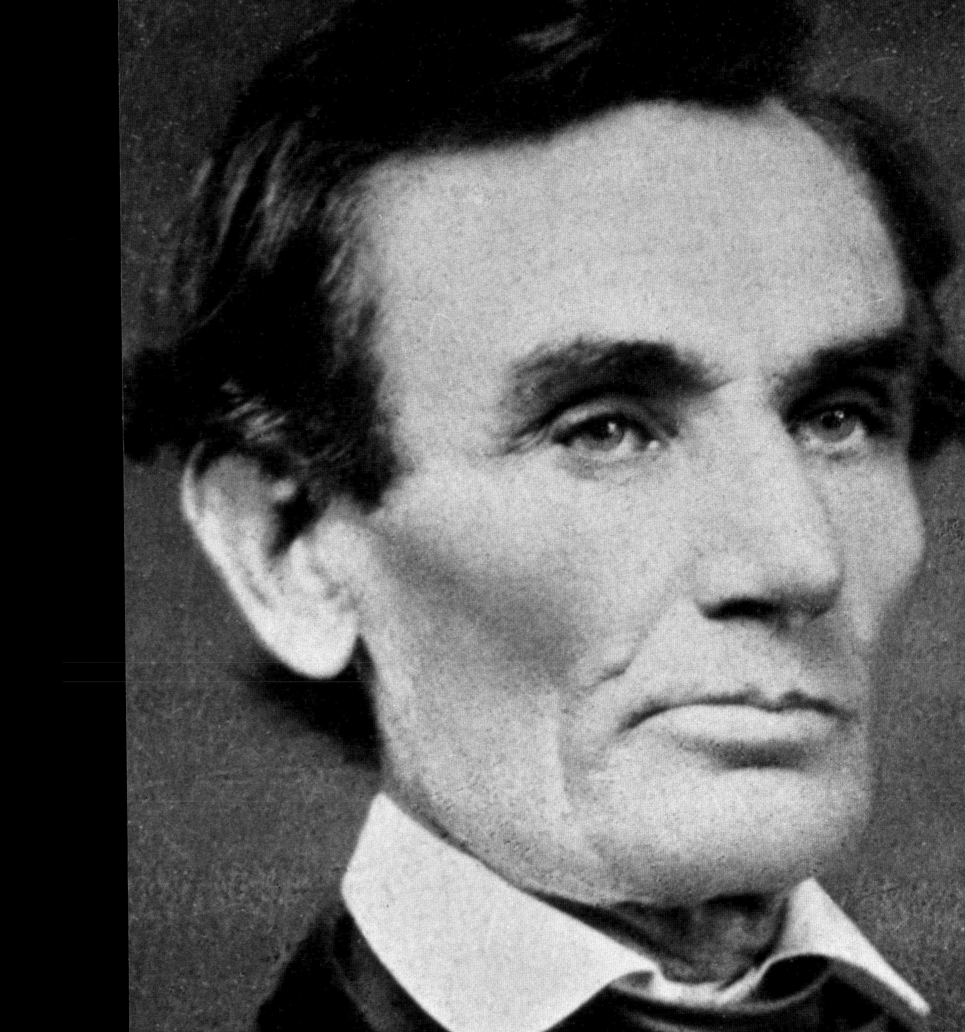

May 7, 1858, *Beardstown, Illinois*

On the same day that he successfully defended Duff Armstrong from murder charges, Lincoln sat for a picture at the studio of eighteen-year-old Abraham Byers, who succinctly recalled the encounter.

He cast his eyes down on his old holland linen suit which had no semblance of starch in it, and said, "These clothes are dirty and unfit for a picture." But I insisted and he finally went with me.

(circa) **July 18, 1858,** *Springfield, Illinois*

AL.1858.3

Photograph by Preston Butler

Within days of having this portrait taken, Lincoln wrote a brief autobiography for inclusion in the Dictionary of Congress.

Born, February 12, 1809, in Hardin County, Kentucky.
Education defective.
Profession, a lawyer.
Have been a captain of volunteers in Black Hawk war.
Postmaster at a very small office.
Four times a member of the Illinois legislature, and was a member of the lower house of Congress. Your, etc.,

A. Lincoln

August 26, 1858, *Macomb, Illinois*

AL.1858.4

Photograph by T. P. Pearson

On the day after this portrait was taken, Lincoln debated Stephen A. Douglas in Freeport, Illinois, where he was observed by journalist Martin P. Rindlaub.

He was swarthy as an Indian, with wiry, jet black hair, which was usually in an unkempt condition. He wore no beard, and his face was almost grotesquely square—he called himself lantern-jawed. His eyes were bright, keen, and of a luminous gray color, though his eyebrows were black like his hair. . . . His figure was gaunt, slender and slightly bent. He was clad in a rusty black Prince Albert coat, with somewhat abbreviated sleeves. His black trousers, too, were so short that they gave an exaggerated size to his feet. He wore a high "stove pipe" hat, somewhat the worse for the wear. He carried a gray woolen shawl.

Possibly **September 26, 1858,** *Springfield, Illinois*

AL.c1858.5

Photograph probably by Christopher S. German

This photograph of Lincoln was taken for his niece Harriet Chapman, who in 1858 lived with her grandmother Sarah Bush Lincoln. Harriet's son, R. N. Chapman, later told the family story of the picture.

In 1858 Lincoln and Douglas had a series of joint debates in this State, and this city was one place of meeting. Mr. Lincoln's stepmother was making her home with my father and mother at the time. Mr. Lincoln stopped at our house, and as he was going away my mother said to him: "Uncle Abe, I want a picture of you." He replied, "Well, Harriet, when I get home I will have one taken for you and send it to you." Soon after, mother received the photograph she still has, already framed, from Springfield, Illinois, with a letter from Mr. Lincoln, in which he said, "This is not a very good-looking picture, but it's the best that could be produced from the poor subject."

October 1, 1858, *Pittsfield, Illinois*

AL.1858.6

Photograph by Calvin Jackson

On a Friday afternoon in the autumn of 1858, Lincoln gave a two-hour speech in the town square of Pittsfield, Illinois, then sat for this portrait by Calvin Jackson. That same day he wrote the following critique of "pro-slavery theology" as it existed in the South and among many northern Democrats.

The sum of pro-slavery theology seems to be this: "Slavery is not universally *right*, nor yet universally *wrong*; it is better for *some* people to be slaves; and, in such cases, it is the Will of God that they be such."

Certainly there is no contending against the Will of God; but still there is some difficulty in ascertaining, and applying it, to particular cases. . . .

But, slavery is good for some people!!! As a *good* thing, slavery is strikingly perculiar, in this, that it is the only good thing which no man ever seeks the good of, *for himself.*

Nonsense! Wolves devouring lambs, not because it is good for their own greedy maws, but because it [is] good for the lambs!!!

October 11, 1858, *Monmouth, Illinois*

Just three days before the sixth debate with Stephen A. Douglas, Lincoln rode into Monmouth, Illinois, where a photographer from thirty miles south in Macomb convinced him to sit for a portrait. The Chicago Tribune *reported that despite heavy rains a large crowd had assembled.*

Of his speech I will only say that it lasted three hours, and that during all that time the whole audience seemed perfectly wrapt in attention, and that in power, pathos and eloquence, I have never heard it equalled. . . . Men who were wavering, old Americans and many Democrats heretofore, were seen to throw up their hats and hurrah for Lincoln.

AL.1858.7

Photograph by William Judkins Thomson

(circa) **1858,** *Location Unknown*

AL.c1858.8

Photographer unknown

Probably around the time this photograph was taken, journalist David R. Locke met Lincoln for the first time in Quincy, Illinois.

I found Mr. Lincoln in a room of a hotel, surrounded by admirers. . . . I succeeded in obtaining an interview with him after the crowd had departed, and I esteem it something to be proud of that he seemed to take a liking to me. He talked to me without reserve. . . . He sat in the room with his boots off, to relieve his very large feet from the pain occasioned by continuous standing; or, to put it in his own words: "I like to give my feet a chance to breathe." He had removed his coat and vest, dropped one suspender from his shoulder, taken off his necktie and collar; and thus comfortably attired, or rather unattired, he sat tilted back in one chair with his feet upon another in perfect ease. He seemed to dislike clothing, and in privacy wore as little of it as he could.

(circa) **1858,** *Springfield, Illinois*

John G. Nicolay, Lincoln's private secretary and biographer, declared this the best photograph he knew of the beardless Lincoln. It was used on a campaign button, and Lincoln's close friend Milton Hay wrote about it.

I am greatly pleased with this picture of Lincoln. I think it reproduces the man as he was, and in the sober expression most habitual with him, better than any other photograph I have seen of him; and this is the opinion of all the old familiar acquaintances of his to whom I have shown it.

AL.c1858.9

Photograph probably by Preston Butler

(circa) **1859,** *Location Unknown*

This portrait was probably taken in 1859, the year that Unitarian minister Moncure Conway first saw Lincoln.

The face had a battered and bronzed look, without being hard. His nose was prominent and buttressed a strong and high forehead; his eyes were high-vaulted and had an expression of sadness; his mouth and chin were too close together, the cheeks hollow. On the whole Lincoln's appearance was not attractive until one heard his voice, which possessed variety of expression, earnestness and shrewdness in every tone. The charm of his manner was that he had no manner; he was simple, direct, humorous.

(circa) **1859,** *probably Springfield, Illinois*

AL.c1859.2

Photographer unknown

In 1859, the year this photograph was probably taken, Lincoln wrote an autobiographical statement for campaign worker Jesse Fell.

I was born Feb. 12, 1809, in Hardin County, Kentucky. My parents were both born in Virginia, of undistinguished families—second families, perhaps I should say. My mother, who died in my tenth year, was of a family of the name of Hanks, some of whom now reside in Adams, and others in Macon counties, Illinois. . . .

My father, at the death of his father, was but six years of age; and he grew up, litterally without education. He removed from Kentucky to what is now Spencer county, Indiana, in my eighth year. We reached our new home about the time the State came into the Union. It was a wild region, with many bears and other wild animals still in the woods. There I grew up. There were some schools, so called; but no qualification was ever required of a teacher, beyond *"readin, writin, and cipherin,"* to the Rule of Three.

October 4, 1859, *Chicago, Illinois*

AL.1859.3

Photograph by Samuel M. Fassett

A month and a half after this photograph was taken, Lincoln wrote this brief physical description of himself.

If any personal description of me is thought desirable, it may be said, I am, in height, six feet, four inches, nearly; lean in flesh, weighing, on an average, one hundred and eighty pounds; dark complexion, with coarse black hair, and grey eyes—no other marks or brands recollected.

February 27, 1860, *New York City*

AL.1860.1

Photograph by Mathew B. Brady

This image became known as the Cooper Union portrait. Made by Mathew Brady on February 27, 1860, it was widely reproduced and spread Lincoln's image across the nation. Richard C. McCormick, a member of the committee in charge of arrangements for Lincoln's Cooper Union address, wrote of the candidate's visit for the New York Evening Post.

We found him in a suit of black, much wrinkled from its careless packing in a small valise. He received us cordially, apologizing for the awkward and uncomfortable appearance he made in his new suit, and expressing himself surprised at being in New York. His form and manner were indeed odd, and we thought him the most unprepossessing public man we had ever met. . . . [I]n a very short time his frank, fluent and sparkling conversation won our hearts and made his plain face pleasant to us all.

We visited a photographic establishment upon the corner of Broadway and Bleecker streets, where he sat for his picture, the first taken in New York. At the gallery he met and was introduced to George Bancroft, and had a brief conversation with that gentleman, who welcomed him to New York. The contrast in the appearance of the men was most striking—the one courtly and precise in his every word and gesture, with the air of a trans-Atlantic statesman; the other bluff and awkward, his very utterance an apology for his ignorance of metropolitan manners and customs. "I am on my way to New Hampshire," he said to Mr. Bancroft, "where I have a son at school, who, if report be true, already knows much more than his father."

May 9, 1860, *Decatur, Illinois*

AL.1860.2

Photograph by Edward A. Barnwell

On May 9, 1860, Lincoln was photographed on the day he addressed a Republican state convention in Decatur, Illinois. At the convention his cousin John Hanks carried two rails into the hall claiming they were from "a lot of 3000 made in 1830" by himself and Lincoln. The sight of the rails gave rise to a spontaneous call for Lincoln to speak, which he did briefly, without a text. The New York Tribune *carried the story.*

He stated that, some thirty years ago, then just emigrating to the State, he stopped with his mother's family, for one season, in what is now Macon County; that he built a cabin, *split rails*, and cultivated a small farm down on the Sangamon River, some six or eight miles from Decatur. These, he was informed, were taken from that fence; but, whether they were or not, he had mauled many and many better ones since he had grown to manhood. The cheers were renewed with the same vigor when he concluded his remarks.

May 20, 1860, *Springfield, Illinois*

AL.1860.3A

Photograph probably by Preston Butler

Governor Marcus L. Ward of New Jersey, a delegate to the 1860 Republican Convention in Chicago, submitted this portrait of Abraham Lincoln for the October 1882 issue of Century Magazine, *where it was published for the first time.*

Sir: I send you with this the ambrotype portrait of our late President Lincoln, to be used in such way as may be the most useful to you. The history of the picture is as follows: On Friday, the 18th of May, 1860, the day succeeding Mr. Lincoln's nomination, I left Chicago for his home in Springfield, for the purpose of congratulating him and forming his personal acquaintance. I was kindly received, and invited to share his hospitalities. . . . On the next day after my arrival,—the 20th—I suggested to Mr. Lincoln that I would like to be the possessor of a good likeness of himself. He replied that he had not a satisfactory picture, "but then," he added, "we will walk out together and I will sit for one." The picture I send you was the result of that sitting. No one, I imagine, will fail to recognize in the expression of the face those noble qualities of the man—honesty, gentleness, and kindness of heart—which so endeared him to all who knew him.

May 20, 1860, *Springfield, Illinois*

Photograph probably by Preston Butler

Lincoln was nominated for the presidency two days before he sat for this photograph and the previous one. Charles Zane was a young lawyer who later joined the practice of Lincoln's law partner William Herndon. He left this description.

I was present in the Illinois State Journal on the day when Lincoln was nominated. . . . L. was cool, but you could see he felt well: Lincoln Said "I must go home: there is a little short woman there that is more interested in this Matter than I am". As Lincoln came down stairs to go home he was met by a number of Irish & American Citizens at the foot of the Stairs at the Journal office, who Congratulated him on the nomination. Mr L said—"Boys you had better come and shake hands with me now that you have an oppertunity—for you do not Know what influence this nomination may have on me. I am human, you Know."

(circa) **May 1860,** *Springfield, Illinois*

AL.1860.4

Photographer unknown

A few months before posing in profile, Lincoln spoke about his childhood with Connecticut minister John P. Gulliver. His words, as Gulliver later reported them, were printed in the Independent.

I never went to school more than six months in my life, but I can say this: that among my earliest recollections I remember how, when a mere child, I used to get irritated when anybody talked to me in a way I could not understand. I do not think I ever got angry at anything else in my life; but that always disturbed my temper; and has ever since. I can remember going to my little bedroom, after hearing the neighbors talk of an evening with my father, and spending no small part of the night walking up and down and trying to make out what was the exact meaning of some of their, to me, dark sayings. I could not sleep, although I tried to, when I got on such a hunt for an idea until I had caught it; and when I thought I had got it, I was not satisfied until I had repeated it over and over; until I had put it in language plain enough, as I thought, for any boy I knew to comprehend. This was a kind of passion with me, and it has stuck by me; for I am never easy now, when I am handling a thought, till I have bounded it north, and bounded it south, and bounded it east, and bounded it west.

June 3, 1860, *Springfield, Illinois*

AL.1860.5A

Photograph by Alexander Hesler

On the same day that Alexander Hesler took this portrait of Lincoln, the artist Charles Barry came to Springfield to sketch the candidate, as he later recalled.

Arriving in Springfield in the afternoon of Saturday, June 3, 1860, I went at once to the Lincoln home. When I rang the bell a very small boy called out: "Hello, Mister, what yer want?" I replied that I wished to see Mr. Lincoln and had come all the way from Boston for that purpose. Then the small boy shouted: "Come down, Pop; here's a man from Boston," and an instant later Mr. Lincoln appeared, holding out a hand in welcome. "They want my head, do they?" he asked, twisting my letter of introduction in his hands. "Well, if you can get it you may have it, that is, if you are able to take it off while I am on the jump; but don't fasten me into a chair. . . ." . . . How vividly it all comes back to me—the lonely room, the great bony figure with its long arms and legs that seemed to be continually twisting themselves together; the long, wiry neck; the narrow chest, the uncombed hair; the cavernous sockets beneath the high forehead; the bushy eyebrows hanging like curtains over the bright, dreamy eyes, the awkward speech, the evident sincerity and patience.

June 3, 1860, *Springfield, Illinois*

AL.1860.5B

Photograph by Alexander Hesler

On the day after sitting for photographer Alexander Hesler, Lincoln wrote a letter to Samuel Haycroft in Kentucky, a slave state.

You suggest that a visit to the place of my nativity might be pleasant to me. Indeed it would. But would it be safe? Would not the people Lynch me?

The place on Knob Creek . . . I remember very well; but I was not born there. As my parents have told me, I was born on Nolin, very much nearer Hodgin's-Mill than the Knob Creek place is. My earliest recollection, however, is of the Knob Creek place.

June 3, 1860, *Springfield, Illinois*

Photograph by Alexander Hesler

During Lincoln's presidential campaign, letters poured in requesting information about him. To George Ashmun of Massachusetts he wrote the following note on June 4, the day after posing for photographer Alexander Hesler.

My dear Sir It seems as if the question whether my first name is "Abraham" or "Abram" will never be settled. It is "*Abraham*" and if the letter of acceptance is not yet in print, you may, if you think fit, have my signature thereto printed "*Abraham Lincoln.*"

Exercise your own judgment about this.

(circa) **June 1860,** *Springfield, Illinois*

AL.1860.6

Photograph by Joseph Hill

About the time he posed for this photograph, Lincoln wrote an autobiographical statement in the third person for a campaign biography.

Abraham Lincoln was born Feb. 12, 1809, then in Hardin, now in the more recently formed county of Larue, Kentucky. His father, Thomas, & grand-father, Abraham, were born in Rockingham county Virginia, whither their ancestors had come from Berks county Pennsylvania. His lineage has been traced no farther back than this. The family were originally quakers, though in later times they have fallen away from the peculiar habits of that people. . . . Abraham, grandfather of the subject of this sketch, came to Kentucky, and was killed by indians about the year 1784. He left a widow, three sons and two daughters. . . . Thomas, the youngest son, and father of the present subject, by the early death of his father, and very narrow circumstances of his mother, even in childhood was a wandering laboring boy, and grew up litterally without education. He never did more in the way of writing than to bunglingly sign his own name.

(circa) **Spring or Summer 1860,** *Illinois*

AL.1860.7

Photographer unknown

This portrait of Lincoln smiling was made for political purposes in 1860 and sent by the candidate to William Bane of Charleston, Illinois. That same spring Lincoln admitted that he wanted to win the presidency, saying, "[T]he taste is in my mouth a little." Writing to a political supporter from Ohio, he described his strategy for winning the nomination.

If I have any chance, it consists mainly in the fact that the *whole* opposition would vote for me if nominated. (I dont mean to include the pro-slavery opposition of the South, of course.) My name is new in the field; and I suppose I am not the *first* choice of a very great many. Our policy, then, is to give no offence to others—leave them in a mood to come to us, if they shall be compelled to give up their first love.

(circa) **Summer 1860,** *Springfield, Illinois*

AL.1860.8

Photograph by William Seavey

In the summer of 1860, when this portrait was taken, Lincoln wrote his old friend and former doctor Anson G. Henry, who had left Springfield eight years earlier for the Oregon Territory. At the end of the letter Lincoln gave an update of the family.

Our boy, in his tenth year, (the baby when you left) has just had a hard and tedious spell of scarlet-fever; and he is not yet beyond all danger. I have a head-ache, and a sore throat upon me now, inducing me to suspect that I have an inferior type of the same thing.

Our eldest boy, Bob, has been away from us nearly a year at school, and will enter Harvard University this month. He promises very well, considering we never controlled him much.

Write again when you receive this. Mary joins in sending our kindest regards to Mrs. H. yourself, and all the family.

Your friend, as ever A. Lincoln

(circa) **Summer 1860,** *probably Springfield, Illinois*

AL.1860.9

Photographer unknown

Lincoln's height was noted by many over the years, including Humphrey W. Carr of Jersey City, New Jersey, who met Lincoln shortly after this full-length portrait was taken.

When my friend and I were announced Mr. Lincoln promptly received us. At our introduction he gave me a cordial grasp of the hand, and I seem now, after many years, to feel the loose joints of his long fingers. He said: "I am glad to meet you, Mr. Carr, and if height has anything in it I have a claim on your vote." . . .

While we were still talking I noticed that he kept looking me up and down as if taking a mental measurement. At last he asked,

"Mr. Carr, how tall *are* you?"

"Six feet two and a half," I replied. "And how tall are you, Mr. Lincoln?"

He straightened up, with a little effort, saying,

"When I *get the kinks all out* I am six feet four inches. Now, Mr. Carr, doesn't that entitle me to your vote?" he asked with a friendly smile as we shook hands in parting.

I did vote for Lincoln—but it was for a better reason than that.

(circa) **Summer 1860,** *probably Springfield, Illinois*

AL.1860.10

Photographer unknown

In the summer of 1860, around the time this photograph was taken, Lincoln wrote the following set of instructions to his personal secretary John G. Nicolay. Lincoln had dispatched him to Indiana to speak with Richard W. Thompson, who had ties to the Know-Nothing Party.

Ascertain what he wants—
On what subject he would converse with me
And the particulars if he will give them—
Is an interview indispensable?
And if so, how soon must it be had?
Tell him my motto is "fairness to all"—
But committ me to nothing.

(circa) **Summer 1860,** *probably Springfield, Illinois*

AL.1860.11

Photograph by William A. Shaw

During the summer of 1860, Lincoln was photographed many times, in response to letters such as this one from Minnesota journalist F. H. Pratt.

A friend of mine at St. Paul's . . . is desirous of procuring an original likeness of yourself, for the purpose of Photographing—copying. The numerous "Wide-Awake-Clubs" that have been formed throughout the State are extremely anxious of having a copy, & I think the idea a good one. By conferring the above favour, you will greatly oblige your numerous friends here and enable them . . . to roll up a handsome majority for the Republican nominee of the Chicago Convention.

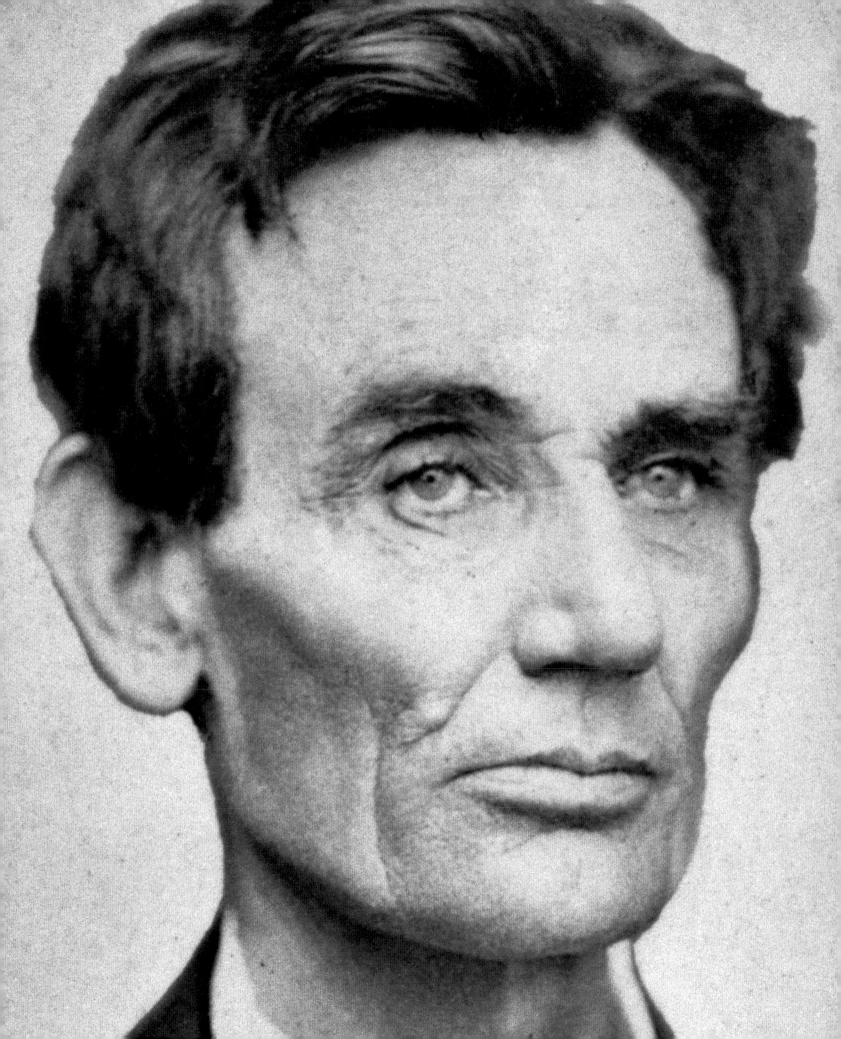

(circa) **Summer 1860,** *probably Springfield, Illinois*

In the summer of 1860, around the time this photograph was taken, Lincoln was forced to deal with a public controversy. A Democratic newspaper quoted him as having spoken out, many years earlier, against Thomas Jefferson, including accusations that the third president had fathered slave children. "The character of Jefferson was repulsive," he had supposedly said. "He brought his own children to the hammer, and made many of his debaucheries." Lincoln, who in fact often spoke kindly of Jefferson and held the Declaration of Independence in the highest regard, sent the following response.

The extract upon a newspaper slip which you sent, and which I herewith return, is a base forgery, so far as its authorship is imputed to me. I never said anything like it, at any time or place. I do not recognize it as anything I have ever seen before, emanating from any source. I wish my name not to be used; but my friends will be entirely safe in denouncing the thing as a forgery, so far as it is ascribed to me.

AL.1860.12

Photographer unknown

August 8, 1860, *Springfield, Illinois*

AL.1860.14

Photograph by William A. Shaw

During the summer of Lincoln's presidential campaign, crowds from a Republican rally followed him back to his house, where he was photographed with them. A reporter with the Peoria Daily Transcript *described the day.*

Immense is the only word that describes today's demonstration. . . . The enthusiasm was beyond all bounds. . . . I never saw so dense and large a crowd. . . . Mr. Lincoln's bearing today, under such a tribute of personal popularity and admiration as I have never before seen paid to any human being, more and more convinces me of the real greatness of his character.

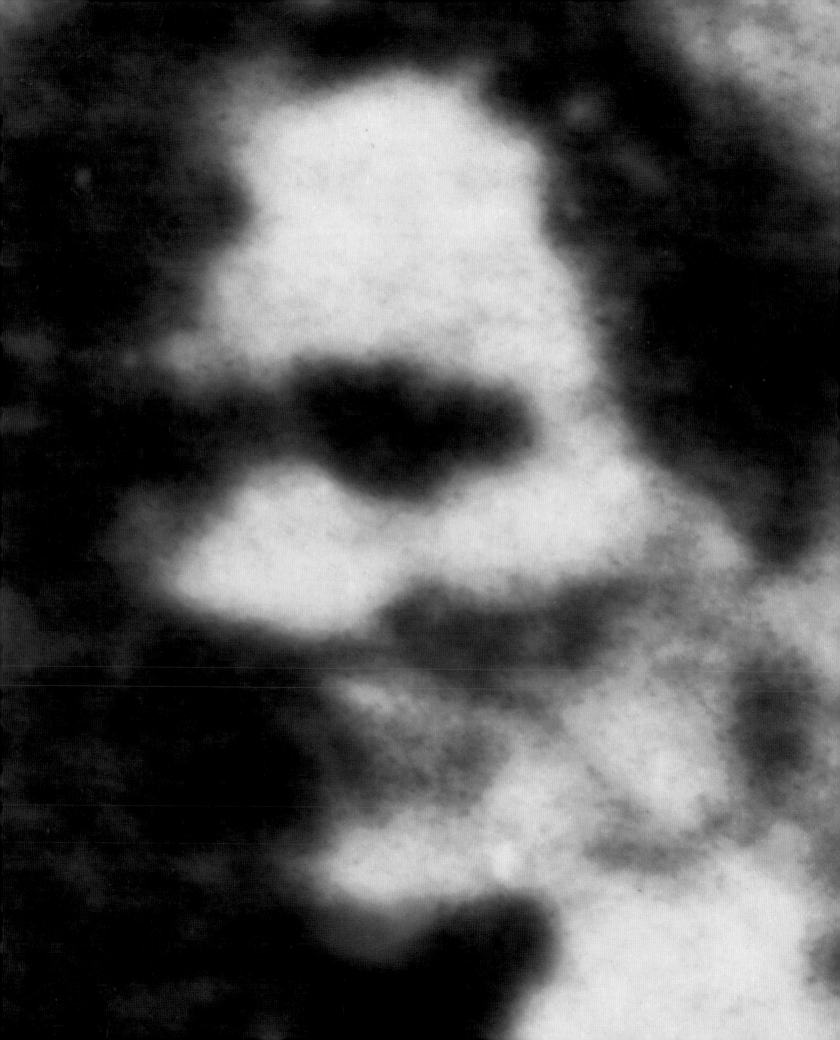

August 13, 1860, *Springfield, Illinois*

AL.1860.15A

Photograph by Preston Butler

This was the last picture taken of Lincoln before his election to the presidency in November 1860. Soon after the contest, journalist Donn Piatt visited him at his home and wrote this description.

Mr. Lincoln was the homeliest man I ever saw. His body seemed to me a huge skeleton in clothes. Tall as he was, his hands and feet looked out of proportion, so long and clumsy were they. Every movement was awkward in the extreme. He sat with one leg thrown over the other, and the pendent foot swung almost to the floor. And all the while two little boys, his sons, clambered over those legs, patted his cheeks, pulled his nose, and poked their fingers in his eyes, without causing reprimand or even notice. He had a face that defied artistic skill to soften or idealize. . . . It was capable of few expressions, but those were extremely striking. When in repose, his face was dull, heavy and repellent. It brightened, like a lit lantern, when animated. His dull eyes would fairly sparkle with fun, or express as kindly a look as I ever saw, when moved by some matter of human interest.

November 25, 1860, *Chicago, Illinois*

AL.1860.16

Photograph by Samuel G. Alschuler

In mid-October 1860 Lincoln received a letter from an eleven-year-old girl from Chautauqua, New York, asking him about his children and suggesting that he grow his whiskers, writing, "You would look a great deal better for your face is so thin." He wrote back the following letter, and five weeks later was photographed with the beginnings of a beard.

My dear little Miss.

Your very agreeable letter of the 15th is received—

I regret the necessity of saying I have no daughters. I have three sons—one seventeen, one nine, and one seven, years of age. They, with their mother, constitute my whole family.

As to the whiskers, having never worn any, do you not think people would call it a piece of silly affect[at]ion if I were to begin it now? Your very sincere well-wisher

A. Lincoln.

(probably) **January 13, 1861,** *Springfield, Illinois*

AL.1861.1

Photograph by Christopher S. German

Just weeks before posing for this portrait, Lincoln wrote to Alexander H. Stephens, in hopes that he would help prevent Georgia from joining the secession.

Do the people of the South really entertain fears that a Republican administration would, *directly, or indirectly*, interfere with their slaves, or with them, about their slaves? If they do, I wish to assure you, as once a friend, and still, I hope, not an enemy, that there is no cause for such fears.

The South would be in no more danger in this respect, than it was in the days of Washington. I suppose, however, this does not meet the case. You think slavery is *right* and ought to be extended; while we think it is *wrong* and ought to be restricted. That I suppose is the rub. It certainly is the only substantial difference between us.

February 9, 1861, *Springfield, Illinois*

AL.1861.2A

Photograph by Christopher S. German

In an 1866 speech, Lincoln's longtime law partner William Herndon described how his friend looked in February 1861.

Abraham Lincoln was about six feet four inches high, and when he left this city was 51 years old, having good health and no gray hairs—or but few in his head. He was thin—tall—wirey—sinewy, grisly—raw boned man, thin through the breast to the back—and narrow across the shoulders, standing he leaned forward—was what may be called stoop shouldered, inclining to the consumptive by build. His usual weight was about 160 pounds. . . . His structure—his build was loose and leathery. His body was shrunk and shrivelled—having dark skin—dark hair—looking woe struck. The whole man— body & mind worked slowly—creekingly, as if it wanted oiling. . . . When Mr. Lincoln walked he moved cautiously, but firmly, his long arms—his hands on them hanging like giants hands, swung down by his side. . . . He was not a pretty man by any means . . . but when that eye and face and every feature were lit up by the inward soul or fire of emotion, *then* it was that all these apparently ugly features sprang to organs of beauty. . . . Sometimes it appeared to me that Lincoln's soul was fresh, just from the presence of its God.

February 9, 1861, *Springfield, Illinois*

AL.1861.2B

Photograph by Christopher S. German

Two days after sitting for this portrait, Lincoln said good-bye to the people of his hometown and departed by train for Washington. Although his farewell address was delivered without a text, Lincoln wrote part of it down in pencil on the train, with John G. Nicolay taking dictation for the rest of it.

My friends. No one, not in my situation, can appreciate my feeling of sadness at this parting. To this place, and the kindness of these people, I owe every thing. Here I have been a quarter of a century, and have passed from a young to an old man. Here my children have been born, and one is buried. I now leave, not knowing when, or whether ever, I may return, with a task before me greater than that which rested upon Washington. Without the assistance of that Divine Being, who ever attended him, I cannot succeed. With that assistance I cannot fail. Trusting in Him, who can go with me, and remain with you and be everywhere for good, let us confidently hope that all will yet be well. To His care commending you, as I hope in your prayers you will commend me, I bid you an affectionate farewell

February 22, 1861, *Philadelphia, Pennsylvania*

AL.1861.3B

Photograph by Frederick DeBourg Richards

En route to his inauguration Lincoln was photographed at a sunrise flag-raising ceremony outside Independence Hall, Philadelphia, immediately following a reception within. He had been warned of the danger of assassination and told that violent mobs awaited him in Baltimore. His words earlier that morning as reported in the Philadelphia Inquirer *focused on the Declaration of Independence.*

I have often inquired of myself, what great principle or idea it was that kept this Confederacy so long together. It was not the mere matter of the separation of the colonies from the mother land; but something in that Declaration giving liberty, not alone to the people of this country, but hope to the world for all future time. (Great applause.) It was that which gave promise that in due time the weights should be lifted from the shoulders of all men, and that *all* should have an equal chance. (Cheers.) This is the sentiment embodied in that Declaration of Independence.

Now, my friends, can this country be saved upon that basis? If it can, I will consider myself one of the happiest men in the world if I can help to save it. . . . But, if this country cannot be saved without giving up that principle—I was about to say I would rather be assassinated on this spot than to surrender it. (Applause.)

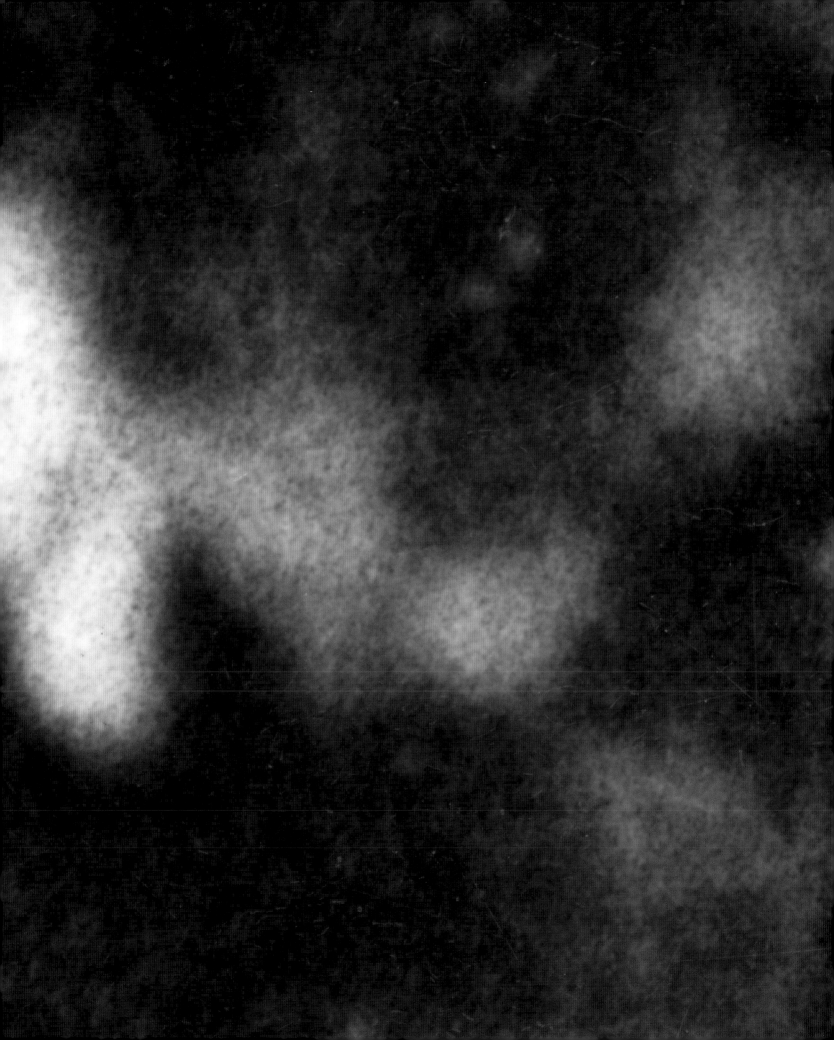

(probably) **February 24, 1861,** *Washington, D.C.*

AL.1861.4A

Photograph by Alexander Gardner

Lincoln arrived in Washington, D.C., on February 23, probably the day before sitting for this portrait. Congressman Elihu Washburne was the first to greet him in the capital city.

I stood behind the pillar awaiting the arrival of the train. When it came to a stop I watched with fear and trembling to see the passengers descend. I saw every car emptied, and there was no Mr. Lincoln. I was well-nigh in despair, and when about to leave I saw slowly emerge from the last sleeping car three persons. I could not mistake the long, lank form of Mr. Lincoln, and my heart bounded with joy and gratitude. He had on a soft low-crowned hat, a muffler around his neck, and a short bob-tailed overcoat. Any one who knew him at that time could not have failed to recognize him at once, but, I must confess, he looked more like a well-to-do farmer from one of the back towns . . . than the President of the United States.

(probably) **February 24, 1861,** *Washington, D.C.*

AL.1861.4C

Photograph by Alexander Gardner

On the day Lincoln most likely sat for this Washington portrait, his secretary John Nicolay wrote a letter to his fiancée.

We all arrived here safely last evening at about 5 o'clock—Mr. Lincoln himself having preceded us the night before. I assure you it was a real pleasure to get to our journey's end—with a prospect of a little rest now and then. During the last week of our trip, in the great whirlpools of New York and Philadelphia, not a moment was our own. . . . For the present we are quartered at Willard's Hotel. The original programme was to go to a private house which had been rented for the purpose. This plan having been changed, and no rooms having been reserved, all the party except Mr. & Mrs. Lincoln have but sorry accommodations. Well, next week we hope to be in the White House, where perhaps it may be better.

You need have no present fears about our entire safety here. There is not the least apprehension about trouble at the inauguration or at any other time. That cloud has blown over.

(circa) **Spring 1861,** *Washington, D.C.*

AL.1861.6B

Photograph possibly by C. D. Fredericks,
James E. McClees, or W. L. German

*Lincoln sent this portrait to the mother of his close friend
Joshua Speed, to whom he had once paid a long visit in
Kentucky. Speed, who later spent time with Lincoln in the
White House, left this description of his friend.*

Mr. Lincoln's person was ungainly. He was six feet four inches in
height; a little stooped in the shoulders; his legs and arms were
long; his feet and hands large; his forehead was high. His head
was over the average size. His eyes were gray. His face and
forehead were wrinkled even in his youth. They deepened in
age, "as streams their channels deeper wear." Generally he
was a very sad man, and his countenance indicated it. But when
he warmed up all sadness vanished, his face was radiant and
glowing, and almost gave expression to his thoughts before his
tongue could utter them. If I was asked what it was that threw
such charm around him, I would say that it was his perfect natu-
ralness. He could act no part but his own.

May 16, 1861, *Washington, D.C.*

AL.1861.7A

Photograph by an unknown operator,
for Mathew B. Brady

A few weeks before this portrait was taken, Lincoln spoke to a fifty-person Baltimore committee that had come urging him to end the war and to stop sending troops through Maryland.

You, gentlemen, come here to me and ask for peace on any terms, and yet have no word of condemnation for those who are making war on us. You express great horror of bloodshed, and yet would not lay a straw in the way of those who are organizing in Virginia and elsewhere to capture this city. The rebels attack Fort Sumter, and your citizens attack troops sent to the defense of the Government, and the lives and property in Washington, and yet you would have me break my oath and surrender the Government without a blow. There is no Washington in that—no Jackson in that—no manhood nor honor in that. I have no desire to invade the South; but I must have troops to defend this Capital. Geographically it lies surrounded by the soil of Maryland; and mathematically the necessity exists that they should come over her territory. Our men are not moles, and can't dig under the earth; they are not birds, and can't fly through the air. There is no way but to march across, and that they must do. But in doing this there is no need of collision. Keep your rowdies in Baltimore, and there will be no bloodshed. Go home and tell your people that if they will not attack us, we will not attack them; but if they do attack us, we will return it, and that severely.

May 16, 1861, *Washington, D.C.*

AL.1861.7C

Photograph by an unknown operator,
for Mathew B. Brady

*British journalist William Howard Russell met Abraham Lin-
coln shortly before he was photographed at Mathew Brady's
Washington studio.*

He was dressed in an ill-fitting, wrinkled suit of black, which put
one in mind of an undertaker's uniform at a funeral; round his
neck a rope of black silk was knotted in a large bulb, with flying
ends projecting beyond the collar of his coat; his turned-down
shirt-collar disclosed a sinewy muscular yellow neck, and above
that, nestling in a great black mass of hair, bristling and com-
pact like a ruff of mourning pins, rose the quaint face and head,
covered with its thatch of wild republican hair . . . ; the mouth is
absolutely prodigious; the lips, straggling and extending almost
from one line of black beard to the other, are only kept in order
by two deep furrows from the nostril to the chin; the nose
itself—a prominent organ—stands out from the face, with an
inquiring, anxious air, as though it were sniffing for some good
thing in the wind; the eyes dark, full, and deeply set, are penetrating, but full of an expression which almost amounts to
tenderness.

May 16, 1861, *Washington, D.C.*

AL.1861.7D

Photograph by an unknown operator,
for Mathew B. Brady

Eight days after this photograph was taken, Lincoln's friend Colonel Elmer Ellsworth was killed in Alexandria, Virginia. Lincoln was devastated upon receiving the news—a reporter found him weeping and unable to speak. The following day Lincoln wrote to the young man's parents.

My dear Sir and Madam, In the untimely loss of your noble son, our affliction here, is scarcely less than your own. So much of promised usefulness to one's country, and of bright hopes for one's self and friends, have rarely been so suddenly dashed, as in his fall. . . . My acquaintance with him began less than two years ago; yet through the latter half of the intervening period, it was as intimate as the disparity of our ages, and my engrossing engagements, would permit. To me, he appeared to have no indulgences or pastimes; and I never heard him utter a profane, or an intemperate word. What was conclusive of his good heart, he never forgot his parents. The honors he labored for so laudably, and, in the sad end, so gallantly gave his life, he meant for them, no less than for himself.

In the hope that it may be no intrusion upon the sacredness of your sorrow, I have ventured to address you this tribute to the memory of my young friend, and your brave and early fallen child.

May God give you that consolation which is beyond all earthly power. Sincerely your friend in a common affliction—

A. Lincoln

May 16, 1861, *Washington, D.C.*

Photograph by an unknown operator,
for Mathew B. Brady

When this profile was taken in May 1861, Lincoln was at work on an address to Congress to explain his rationale for fighting the Civil War. It was published six weeks later.

This is essentially a People's contest. On the side of the Union, it is a struggle for maintaining in the world, that form, and substance of government, whose leading object is, to elevate the condition of men—to lift artificial weights from all shoulders—to clear the paths of laudable pursuit for all—to afford all, an unfettered start, and a fair chance, in the race of life. . . . I am most happy to believe that the plain people understand, and appreciate this.

May 16, 1861, *Washington, D.C.*

AL.1861.7F

Photograph by an unknown operator,
for Mathew B. Brady

Just weeks before this portrait was taken, Lincoln issued a proclamation declaring the blockade of Southern ports. Journalist Charles Godfrey Leland later commented on his moderate stance toward the border states.

It is certain that by his humane and wise policy, which many attributed to cowardice, President Lincoln not only prevented much bloodshed and devastation, but also preserved the State of Maryland. In such a crisis harshly aggressive measures in Maryland would have irritated millions on the border, and perhaps have brought the war farther north.

(circa) **September 1861,** *Washington, D.C.*

On the issue of slavery Lincoln was a moderate, refusing in 1861 to make emancipation a war aim and focusing strictly on saving the Union. Nor would he agree to include blacks in the Union Army. This put him into conflict with abolitionists, and shortly before this photograph was taken Frederick Douglass wrote a fiery editorial.

Why does the Government reject the negro? Is he not a man? Can he not wield a sword, fire a gun, march and countermarch, and obey orders like any other? . . . If persons so humble as we can be allowed to speak to the President of the United States, we . . . would tell him that this is no time to fight with one hand, when both are needed; that this is no time to fight with only your white hand, and allow your black hand to remain tied. . . . [W]hile the Government continues to refuse the aid of colored men, thus alienating them from the national cause, and giving rebels the advantage of them, it will not deserve better fortunes than it has thus far experienced.—Men in earnest don't fight with one hand, when they might fight with two, and a man drowning would not refuse to be saved even by a colored hand.

October 3, 1862, *Antietam, Maryland*

AL.1862.1B

Photograph by Alexander Gardner

In the summer of 1862, Lincoln decided to issue the Emancipation Proclamation, but agreed to hold back until a Northern victory. That victory came on September 17 at Antietam in Maryland. Five days later he issued the Preliminary Proclamation, then traveled to the battlefield. The artist Francis Carpenter reported Lincoln's account of how it all happened.

It had got to be midsummer, 1862. Things had gone from bad to worse, until I felt that we had reached the end of our rope on the plan of operations we had been pursuing. . . . I now determined upon the adoption of the emancipation policy; and, without consultation with, or the knowledge of the Cabinet, I prepared the original draft of the proclamation, and, after much anxious thought, called a Cabinet meeting upon the subject. . . . Secretary Seward spoke. He said in substance . . . "[W]hile I approve the measure, I suggest, sir, that you postpone its issue, until you can give it to the country supported by military success, instead of issuing it, as would be the case now, upon the greatest disasters of the war!" . . . The result was that I put the draft of the proclamation aside, as you do with a sketch for a picture, waiting for a victory. From time to time I added or changed a line, touching it up here and there, anxiously watching the progress of events. . . . Finally came the week of the battle of Antietam. I determined to wait no longer.

October 3, 1862, *Antietam, Maryland*

AL.1862.1C

Photograph by Alexander Gardner

As part of Lincoln's tour of the battlefield, he visited Confederate wounded in Sharpsburg, as a Baltimore journalist reported.

Passing through one of the hospitals devoted exclusively to Confederate sick and wounded, President Lincoln's attention was drawn to a young Georgian—a fine noble looking youth—stretched upon a humble cot. He was pale, emaciated and anxious, far from kindred and home, vibrating, as it were, between life and death. Every stranger that entered [was] caught in his restless eyes, in hope of their being some relative or friend. President Lincoln observed this youthful soldier, approached and spoke, asking him if he suffered much pain. "I do," was the reply. "I have lost a leg, and feel I am sinking from exhaustion." "Would you," said Mr. Lincoln, "shake hands with me if I were to tell you who I am?" The response was affirmative. "There should," remarked the young Georgian, "be no enemies in this place." Then said the distinguished visitor, "I am Abraham Lincoln, President of the United States." The young sufferer raised his head, looking amazed, and freely extended his hand, which Mr. Lincoln took and pressed tenderly for some time. There followed an instinctive pause. The wounded Confederate's eyes melted into tears; his lips quivered, and his heart beat full. President Lincoln bent over him motionless and dumb. His eyes, too, were overflowing.

October 3, 1862, *Antietam, Maryland*

AL.1862.1E

Photograph by Alexander Gardner

During his visit to Army Headquarters, Lincoln met privately with General George B. McClellan in his tent. Ten days later he sent his general the following message.

You remember my speaking to you of what I called your over-cautiousness. Are you not over-cautious when you assume that you can not do what the enemy is constantly doing? Should you not claim to be at least his equal in prowess, and act upon the claim? . . . You dread his going into Pennsylvania. But if he does so in full force, he gives up his communications to you absolutely, and you have nothing to do but to follow, and ruin him; if he does so with less than full force, fall upon, and beat what is left behind all the easier. . . . In coming to us, he tenders us an advantage which we should not waive. We should not so operate as to merely drive him away. As we must beat him somewhere, or fail finally, we can do it, if at all, easier near to us, than far away. If we can not beat the enemy where he now is, we never can. . . .

August 9, 1863, *Washington, D.C.*

AL.1863.1A

Photograph by Alexander Gardner

For ten months during 1862 and 1863 no photograph was taken of Abraham Lincoln. But a month after the Battle of Gettysburg, his secretary John Hay accompanied the President to Gardner's photography studio. Two days earlier Hay had written about Lincoln in a letter to John Nicolay, referring to him, as he often did, as the Tycoon.

The Tycoon is in fine whack. I have rarely seen him more serene & busy. He is managing this war, the draft, foreign relations, and planning a reconstruction of the Union, all at once. I never knew with what tyrannous authority he rules the Cabinet, till now. The most important things he decides & there is no cavil. I am growing more and more firmly convinced that the good of the country absolutely demands that he should be kept where he is till this thing is over. There is no man in the country, so wise[,] so gentle and so firm. I believe the hand of God placed him where he is.

August 9, 1863, *Washington, D.C.*

AL.1863.1E

Photograph by Alexander Gardner

The day after Lincoln sat for this portrait—his favorite of the group of pictures taken that day—he was introduced to his longtime critic Frederick Douglass, who wanted to speak to him about the treatment of captured black soldiers in the South. Just four months later Douglas spoke about the meeting.

When I went in the President was sitting in his usual position, I was told, with his feet in different parts of the room, taking it easy. As I came in and approached him, the President began to rise, and he continued to rise until he stood over me; and he reached out his hand and said, "Mr. Douglass, I know you; I have read about you, and Mr. Seward has told me about you;" putting me at ease at once. . . . I never met with a man, who . . . impressed me more entirely with his sincerity, with his devotion to his country, and with his determination to save it at all hazards. . . . [T]he President said to me, "Mr. Douglass I have been charged with being tardy and . . . with vacillating; but . . . I think it cannot be shown that when I have once taken a position, I have ever retreated from it." That I regarded as the most significant point in what he said during our interview.

August 9, 1863, *Washington, D.C.*

The day before standing for this photograph Lincoln wrote a letter to his wife, Mary, who was on vacation in New Hampshire recovering from a carriage accident and spending time with her sons Robert and Tad.

My dear Wife. All as well as usual, and no particular trouble any way. I put the money into the Treasury at five per cent, with the previlege of withdrawing it any time upon thirty days' notice. I suppose you are glad to learn this. Tell dear Tad, poor "Nanny Goat," is lost; and Mrs. Cuthbert & I are in distress about it. The day you left Nanny was found resting herself, and chewing her little cud, on the middle of Tad's bed. But now she's gone! The gardener kept complaining that she destroyed the flowers, till it was concluded to bring her down to the White House. This was done, and the second day she had disappeared, and has not been heard of since. This is the last we know of poor "Nanny."

AL.1863.1F

Photograph by Alexander Gardner

August 9, 1863, *Washington, D.C.*

AL.1863.1G

Photograph by Alexander Gardner

Two weeks after this portrait was taken, Lincoln wrote about his policy toward black soldiers and their freedom.

Peace does not appear so distant as it did. I hope it will come soon, and come to stay; and so come as to be worth the keeping in all future time. It will then have been proved that, among free men, there can be no successful appeal from the ballot to the bullet; and that they who take such appeal are sure to lose their case, and pay the cost. And then, there will be some black men who can remember that, with silent tongue, and clenched teeth, and steady eye, and well-poised bayonet, they have helped mankind on to this great consummation; while, I fear, there will be some white ones, unable to forget that, with malignant heart, and deceitful speech, they have strove to hinder it.

November 8, 1863, *Washington, D.C.*

AL.1863.2A

Photograph by Alexander Gardner

Both John Nicolay and John Hay, Lincoln's personal secretaries, prized this photograph of the three of them. Hay (on right) wrote about it in his diary.

Went with Mrs. Ames to Gardner's Gallery & were soon joined by Nico and the Prest. We had a great many pictures taken. Some of the Prest, the best I have seen. Nico and I immortalized ourselves by having ourselves done in group with the Prest.

November 8, 1863, *Washington, D.C.*

AL.1863.2B

Photograph by Alexander Gardner

When this portrait of Abraham Lincoln was taken, he was still planning his address for Gettysburg, to be delivered eleven days later. No one knows for sure when and where Lincoln actually wrote the address, but his secretary John Nicolay speculated.

There is no decisive record of when Mr. Lincoln wrote the first sentences of his proposed address. He probably followed his usual habit in such matters, using great deliberation in arranging his thoughts, and molding his phrases mentally, waiting to reduce them to writing until they had taken satisfactory form.

November 8, 1863, *Washington, D.C.*

AL.1863.2D

Photograph by Alexander Gardner

Less than two weeks before this photograph was taken, Lincoln intervened in the case of a young soldier being court-martialed for conduct unbecoming. Captain James Madison Cutts, Jr., had quarreled with a fellow officer and been caught looking through a keyhole at a woman undressing. Lincoln overturned the military court's verdict and wrote Cutts some fatherly advice.

Although what I am now to say is to be, in form, a reprimand, it is not intended to add a pang to what you have already suffered upon the subject to which it relates. You have too much of life yet before you, and have shown too much of promise as an officer, for your future to be lightly surrendered. You were convicted of two offences. One of them, not of great enormity, and yet greatly to be avoided, I feel sure you are in no danger of repeating. The other you are not so well assured against. The advice of a father to his son "Beware of entrance to a quarrel, but being in, bear it that the opposed may beware of thee," is good, and yet not the best. Quarrel not at all. No man resolved to make the most of himself, can spare time for personal contention. Still less can he afford to take all the consequences, including the vitiating of his temper, and the loss of self-control. . . . Better give your path to a dog, than be bitten by him in contesting for the right. Even killing the dog would not cure the bite.

November 8, 1863, *Washington, D.C.*

AL.1863.2E

Photograph by Alexander Gardner

Nine days after this photograph was taken, Lincoln was still seeking out resources that would help inspire his words for the Gettysburg Address. William Saunders worked in the Agriculture Department and had designed the cemetery for Gettysburg. He later left this recollection.

A few days before the dedication of the grounds, President Lincoln sent word to me that he desired me to call at his office on the evening of the 17th, and take with me the plan of the cemetery. I was on hand at the appointed time, and spread the plan on his office table. He took much interest in it, asked about its surroundings, about Culp's Hill, Round Top, etc., and seemed familiar with the topography of the place although he had never been there. He was much pleased with the method of the graves, said it differed from the ordinary cemetery, and, after I had explained the reasons, said it was an advisable and benefitting arrangement.

November 19, 1863, *Gettysburg, Pennsylvania*

AL.1863.3

Photographer unknown, possibly David Bachrach

An enlargement from this crowd shot at Gettysburg reveals the face of Lincoln not far beneath the distant tree. Thirteen-year-old David R. Shriver was in the crowd that day when Lincoln delivered his Gettysburg Address.

When President Lincoln was introduced I felt a thrill go through me. My father told me to pay close attention as the President would no doubt have something important to say. The people became so still when Mr. Lincoln came before them that you could hear the slightest sound. He looked pale and worried but there was a friendliness about his attitude that immediately won the admiration of those assembled. You could hear the flutter of the paper as he reached inside his coat pocket and brought out his address.

There was a tenseness everywhere as he spoke and in some eyes I thought I saw a trace of tears. When the President had concluded there wasn't a sound. The people had no doubt expected him to speak longer. But the silence was only for a few moments. When they realized he had finished they broke out into cheers. . . . When the demonstration had died down somewhat, Dr. Everett came forward again. "I would freely give the forty pages of my address," he said, "for the twenty lines spoken by President Lincoln. What he has said will never die. I believe those words will never die."

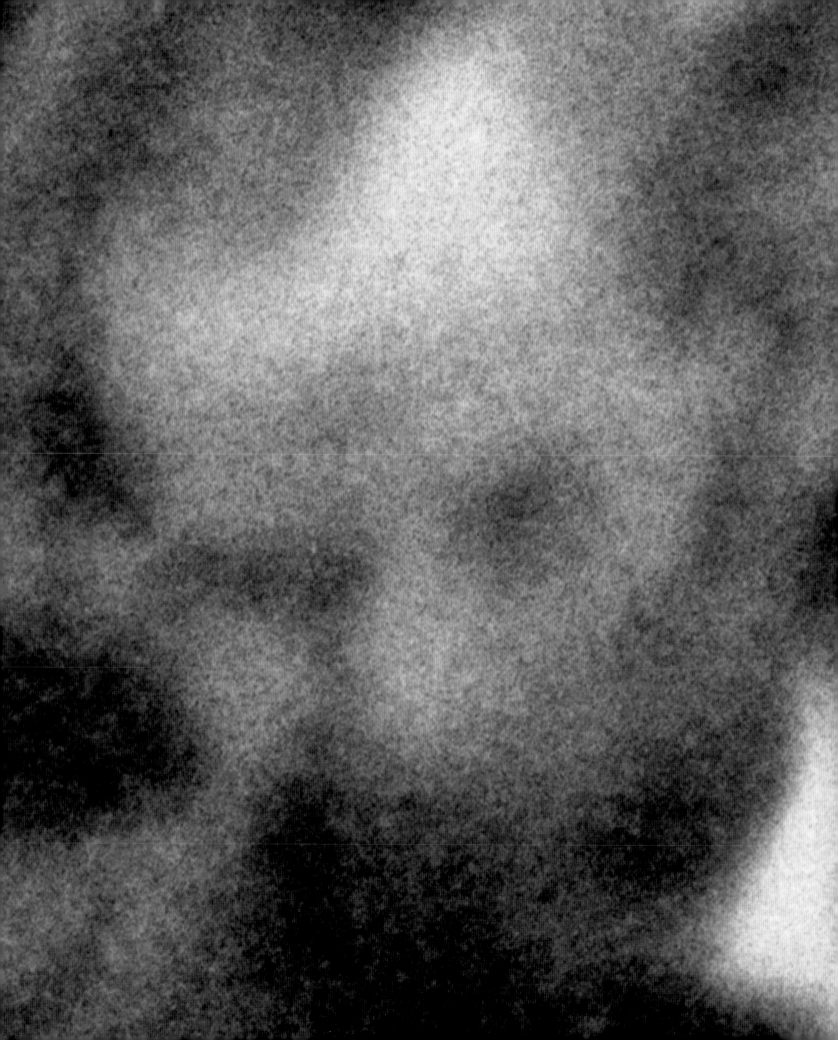

(circa) **1863,** *Washington, D.C.*

AL.c1863.4

Photograph by Lewis Emory Walker

On the day after delivering his Gettysburg Address, Lincoln received a letter from Edward Everett, the main speaker of the day. "I should be glad," Everett wrote, "if I could flatter myself that I came as near to the central idea of the occasion, in two hours, as you did in two minutes." In response Lincoln wrote the following letter.

My dear Sir:

Your kind note of to-day is received. In our respective parts yesterday, you could not have been excused to make a short address, nor I a long one. I am pleased to know that, in your judgment, the little I did say was not entirely a failure. Of course I knew Mr. Everett would not fail; and yet, while the whole discourse was eminently satisfactory, and will be of great value, there were passages in it which trancended my expectation. The point made against the theory of the general government being only an agency, whose principals are the States, was new to me, and, as I think, is one of the best arguments for the national supremacy. The tribute to our noble women for their angel-ministering to the suffering soldiers, surpasses, in its way, as do the subjects of it, whatever has gone before.

Our sick boy, for whom you kindly inquire, we hope is past the worst.

Your Obt. Servt. A. Lincoln

January 8, 1864, *Washington, D.C.*

AL.1864.1A

Photograph by Mathew B. Brady

Over the course of his presidency Lincoln received many warnings and death threats. Around the time he sat for this portrait, the following letter arrived in his daily mail.

New York

Jan 4th/64

Abm Lincoln President,

The same who warned you of a conspiracy, Novr 18th 1862. is now compelled to inform you, that, "Your days are numbered", you have been weighed in the balance & found wanting.—You shall be a dead man in six months from date Dec. 31 1863.

Thus saith the good Spirit.

Joseph.

January 8, 1864, *Washington, D.C.*

AL.1864.1B

Photograph by Mathew B. Brady

On the day that this photograph was taken, Lincoln wrote to a Pittsburgh widow named Esther Stockton, the grandmother of four officers in the Union Army, who had knitted socks for Federal soldiers.

Madam: Learning that you who have passed the eighty-fourth year of life, have given to the soldiers, some three hundred pairs of stockings, knitted by yourself, I wish to offer you my thanks. Will you also convey my thanks to those young ladies who have done so much in feeding our soldiers while passing through your city?

Yours truly,
A. Lincoln

January 8, 1864, *Washington, D.C.*

AL.1864.1D

Photograph by Mathew B. Brady

On the evening after this picture was taken, Lincoln's secretary of the navy, Gideon Welles, described that day's cabinet meeting.

To-day at the Executive Mansion. Only Usher with myself was present, and no business transacted. Mr. Hudson of Massachusetts, formerly Member of Congress, was with the President. Conversation was general, with anecdotes as usual. These are usually very appropriate and instructive, conveying much truth in few words, well, if not always elegantly, told. The President's estimate of character is usually very correct, and he frequently divests himself of partiality with a readiness that has surprised me.

January 8, 1864, *Washington, D.C.*

AL.1864.1E

Photograph by Mathew B. Brady

Of the thousands of letters that Lincoln received during his presidency, many were requests for personal favors. The day after sitting for this portrait, Lincoln was sent a plea from a Southern woman, Eva Young, about her brother.

Mr President

You can Scarcely imagine how very formidable to me is the thought of attempting to write to you the Chief Magistrate of our Country, but when I remember how kind your noble heart is, and how attentively you listened to my earnest appeal in my brothers behalf, then I feel Confidence in addressing you once more on this subject which is so near my heart. . . . May I a true and *loyal Georgian*, ask that my Brother, Col Watkins may be appointed from that State, where for his loyalty and activity in the good cause, he is stigmatized as a "renegade" The noble Kentucky Troops whom he now has the honour of Commanding, would serve with him as cheerfully then as now.

February 9, 1864, *Washington, D.C.*

AL.1864.2A

Photograph by Anthony Berger

The artist Francis Carpenter wrote an account of Lincoln on the day he sat for the portrait that would later serve as the model for the image on the U.S. penny.

At three o'clock the President was to accompany me, by appointment, to Brady's photographic galleries on Pennsylvania Avenue. The carriage had been ordered, and Mrs. Lincoln, who was to accompany us, had come down at the appointed hour, dressed for the ride, when one of those vexations, incident to all households, occurred. Neither carriage [n]or coachman was to be seen. The President and myself stood upon the threshold of the door under the portico, awaiting the result of the inquiry for the coachman, when a letter was put into his hand. While he was reading this, people were passing, as is customary, up and down the promenade, which leads through the grounds to the War Department, crossing, of course, the portico. My attention was attracted to an approaching party, apparently a countryman, plainly dressed, with his wife and two little boys, who had evidently been straying about, looking at the places of public interest in the city. As they reached the portico, the father, who was in advance, caught sight of the tall figure of Mr. Lincoln, absorbed in his letter. His wife and the little boys were ascending the steps. The man stopped suddenly, put out his hand with a "hush" to his family, and, after a moment's gaze, he bent down and whispered to them, — "There is the President!" Then leaving them, he slowly made a half circuit around Mr. Lincoln, watching him intently all the while. At this point, having finished his letter, the President turned to me, and said: "Well, we will not wait any longer for the carriage; it won't hurt you and me to walk down."

February 9, 1864, *Washington, D.C.*

AL.1864.2B

Photograph by Anthony Berger

On the day Lincoln sat for this portrait, the daughter of an old friend wrote about her father who had been convicted of smuggling ammunition across Confederate lines. In late March, partly in response to this letter, Lincoln granted Henry Luckett a full pardon.

Dear Sir

I have taken the liberty of writing to you in behalf of my Father whose case you have had presented to you before he has been in prison for seven months and is now just recovering from an attack of billious fever he is very feble and unless he is released will die Oh Mr Lincoln it is enough to break my heart to see his situation broken in mind and body. my only dependence three little Orphan Grandchildren depending on him for bread to put in their mouths we have no other means of surport. . . . [I]s he to lay in prison and die; Oh Mr Lincoln you have a heart a kind heart then for my sake and those little Motherless Children have mercy on him and release him he is ready and willing to give bond think of his age nearly 70 years old his ill health impaired mind and I know you will pity and release him in your hands . . .

Yours respectfully

Hattie L Luckett

February 9, 1864, *Washington, D.C.*

AL.1864.2C

Photograph by Anthony Berger

This letter, written to Lincoln the same week he was photographed, is just one of an array of diverse requests that came across his desk each day.

Sir—At the Sanitary Fair to be held in Brooklyn the 22nd inst there is to be a New England department for which, among other things in the artistic line, Specimens in Hair work are solicited.

Mrs Penfield wishes to contribute in that line, and to make a long story short, she wishes a lock of the Presidents hair, also of Mrs Lincoln's—then the specimen would have substantial worth. As no other Hair would be used in connection, pretty good locks & long, would be needed

An autograph letter from President Lincoln certifying to the genuineness &c would be invaluable.

February 9, 1864, *Washington, D.C.*

AL.1864.2D

Photograph by Anthony Berger

A day after sitting for this photograph, Lincoln noticed smoke coming from the grounds of the executive mansion. White House guard Smith Stimmel recorded what happened next.

Just then the front door of the White House flew open with a jerk, and out came the President buttoning his coat around him, and said to me, "Where is the fire, what's burning?" I said, "It seems to be around in the vicinity of the stable." With that he started off on a dog-trot down the steps and along the way leading to the stable. When he started to go to the fire, I thought to myself, "Old fellow, you are the man we are guarding, guess I'll go along." So I struck out on the double-quick and went with him, keeping close to his side; but he took such long strides that his dog-trot was almost a dead run for me. As soon as we got around where we could see what was burning, we saw that, sure enough, the White House stable was on fire. . . . Mr. Lincoln asked hastily if the horses had been taken out, and when told they had not, he rushed through the crowd and began to break open one of the larger doors with his own hands; but the building was full of fire, and none of the horses could be saved.

February 9, 1864, *Washington, D.C.*

AL.1864.2E

Photograph by Anthony Berger

Ten-year-old Tad Lincoln accompanied his father to Brady's Gallery in February, and the two of them were photographed together reading a book. When the picture was widely reproduced, Lincoln told his friend Noah Brooks that he worried it would be misinterpreted.

Lincoln explained to me that he was afraid that this picture was a species of false pretense. Most people, he thought, would suppose the book a large clasped Bible, whereas it was a big photograph album which the photographer, posing the father and son, had hit upon as a good device to use in this way to bring the two sitters together. Lincoln's anxiety lest somebody should think he was "making believe [to] read the Bible to Tad," was illustrative of his scrupulous honesty.

February 9, 1864, *Washington, D.C.*

AL.1864.2F

Photograph by Anthony Berger

Six days after posing for this photograph at Mathew Brady's studio, Lincoln wrote to Major General Daniel Sickles, who had lost his leg at Gettysburg, asking him to undertake a special mission.

I wish you to make a tour for me (principally for observation and information) by way of Cairo and New-Orleans, and returning by the Gulf and Ocean. All Military and Naval officers are to facilitate you with suitable transportation, and by conferring with you, and imparting, so far as they can, the information herein indicated, but you are not to command any of them. . . . [L]earn what you can as to the colored people—how they get along as soldiers, as laborers in our service, on leased plantations, and as hired laborers with their old masters, if there be such cases. Also learn what you can about the colored people within the rebel lines. Also get any other information you may consider interesting, and, from time to time, send me what you may deem important to be known here at once, and be ready to make a general report on your return.

Yours truly
A. Lincoln

(circa) **1864,** *Washington, D.C.*

In 1864 Lincoln spoke these memorable words to the 166th Ohio Regiment.

It is not merely for to-day, but for all time to come that we should perpetuate for our children's children this great and free government, which we have enjoyed all our lives. I beg you to remember this, not merely for my sake, but for yours. I happen temporarily to occupy this big White House. I am a living witness that any one of your children may look to come here as my father's child has. It is in order that each of you may have through this free government which we have enjoyed, an open field and a fair chance for your industry, enterprise and intelligence; that you may all have equal privileges in the race of life, with all its desirable human aspirations. It is for this the struggle should be maintained, that we may not lose our birthright—not only for one, but for two or three years. The nation is worth fighting for, to secure such an inestimable jewel.

AL.c1864.3B

Photograph by an unknown operator,
for Wenderoth & Taylor

April 20, 1864, *Washington, D.C.*

Photograph by Anthony Berger

Ten days after he sat for this portrait—the glass negative of which was later broken— Lincoln was described by John Hay in a diary entry.

A little after midnight as I was writing those last lines, the President came into the office laughing, with a volume of Hood's works in his hand to show Nicolay & me the little Caricature "An unfortunate Bee-ing," seemingly utterly unconscious that he with his short shirt hanging about his long legs & setting out behind like the tail feathers of an enormous ostrich was infinitely funnier than anything in the book he was laughing at. What a man it is! Occupied all day with matters of vast moment, deeply anxious about the fate of the greatest army of the world, with his own fame & future hanging on the events of the passing hour, he yet has such a wealth of simple bonhommie & good fellow ship that he gets out of bed & perambulates the house in his shirt to find us that we may share with him the fun of one of poor Hoods queer little conceits.

April 26, 1864, *Washington, D.C.*

AL.1864.5A

Photograph by Anthony Berger

White House artist Francis Carpenter arranged for this candid photograph to be taken in Lincoln's office and later wrote about it.

The day after the review of Burnside's division, some photographers from Brady's Gallery came up to the White House to make some stereoscopic studies for me of the President's office. They requested a dark closet, in which to develop the pictures; and without a thought that I was infringing upon anybody's rights, I took them to an unoccupied room of which little "Tad" had taken possession a few days before . . . Everything went on well, and one or two pictures had been taken, when suddenly there was an uproar. The operator came back to the office and said that "Tad" had taken great offence at the occupation of his room without his consent, and had locked the door, refusing all admission. . . . In the midst of this conversation, "Tad" burst in, in a fearful passion. He laid all the blame upon me,—said that I had no right to use his room, and that the men should not go in even to get their things. . . . Mr. Lincoln had been sitting for a photograph, and was still in the chair. He said, very mildly, "Tad, go and unlock the door." . . . [A]nd then, suddenly rising, he strode across the passage with the air of one bent on punishment, and disappeared in the domestic apartments. Directly he returned with the key to the theatre, which he unlocked himself. "There," said he, "go ahead, it is all right now." He then went back to his office, followed by myself, and resumed his seat. "Tad," said he, half apologetically, . . . "was violently excited when I went to him. I said, 'Tad, do you know you are making your father a great deal of trouble?' He burst into tears, instantly giving me up the key."

April 26, 1864, *Washington, D.C.*

AL.1864.5C

Photograph by Anthony Berger

"The end of the table on which his hand and book rests," wrote Francis Carpenter; "is the historic table . . . where the Proclamation of Emancipation was signed." Lincoln's friend and biographer Isaac Arnold left the following description of this famous room.

His reception-room—which he called his office—was on the second floor on the south side of the White House. . . . In the center, on the west, was a large white marble fire-place, with big old-fashioned brass andirons, and a large and high brass fender. A wood fire was burning in cool weather. The large windows opened on the beautiful lawn to the south, with a view of the unfinished Washington Monument, the Smithsonian Institute, the Potomac, Alexandria, and down the river towards Mt. Vernon. . . . The furniture of this room consisted of a large oak table . . . extending north and south, and it was around this table that the Cabinet sat when it held its meetings. . . . A tall desk with pigeon-holes for papers stood against the south wall. The only books usually found in this room were the Bible, the United States Statutes, and a copy of Shakespeare. There were a few chairs, and two plain hair-covered sofas. . . . There was an old and discolored engraving of General Jackson on the mantel. . . . Here, in this plain room, Mr. Lincoln spent most of his time while President. Here he received every one, from the Chief Justice and Lieutenant General to the private soldier and humblest citizen.

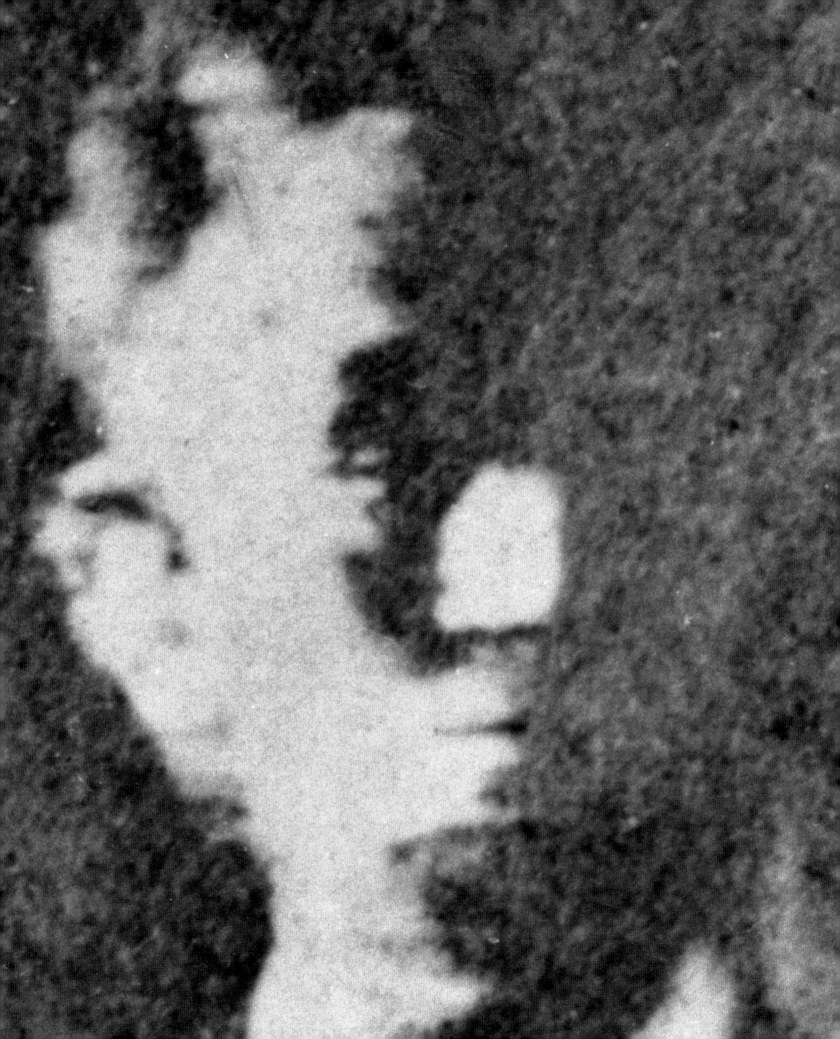

February 5, 1865, *Washington, D.C.*

AL.1865.1A

Photograph by Alexander Gardner

Not long before this portrait of Lincoln and Tad was taken, journalist Russell Conwell paid a visit to the White House. He found Lincoln exhausted but also thinking of the future. At one point, Conwell said, his "face beamed as he rose from his chair" to speak.

When this war is over—and that won't be long—I tell my boy Tad that we will go back to the farm, where I was happier as a boy when I dug potatoes at twenty-five cents a day than I am now; I tell him I will buy him a mule and a pony and he shall have a little cart and he shall make a little garden in a field all his own. . . . Yes, I will be far happier than I have ever been here.

February 5, 1865, *Washington, D.C.*

AL.1865.1D

Photograph by Alexander Gardner

At the time Lincoln sat for this photograph he was exultant over the recent passage of the Thirteenth Amendment. That winter he had worked hard to line up votes for it in Congress, as Massachusetts congressman John B. Alley recalled.

Mr. Lincoln was a thorough and most adroit politician as well as statesman, and in politics always adopted the means to the end, fully believing that in vital issues, "success was a duty." . . . I need only refer to his action and conduct in procuring the passage of the constitutional amendment abolishing slavery. It required a two-thirds vote of Congress to enable the amendments to the Constitution . . . and there were two votes lacking to make two-thirds. . . . Two members of the House were sent for and Mr. Lincoln said . . . "The abolition of slavery by constitutional provision settles the fate, for all coming time, not only of the millions now in bondage, but of unborn millions to come—a measure of such importance that *those two votes must be procured.* I leave it to you to determine how it shall be done; but . . . I expect you to procure those votes."

February 5, 1865, *Washington, D.C.*

AL.1865.1E

Photograph by Alexander Gardner

Three days before this photograph was taken, New York clergy-man Henry Ward Beecher met with Lincoln in the White House.

We were alone in the receiving-room. His hair was "every way for Sunday." It looked as though it was an abandoned stubble field. He had on slippers, and his vest was what was called "going free." He looked wearied, and when he sat down in a chair, looked as though every limb wanted to drop off his body. . . . When [my sister] Mrs. Stowe called to see Lincoln towards the close of the war, she says that she spoke of the great relief he must feel at the prospect of . . . the establishment of peace. And he said, in a sad way, "No, Mrs. Stowe, I shall never live to see peace; this war is killing me;" and he had a presentiment that he would not live long, that he had put his whole life into the war, and that when it was over he would then collapse.

(circa) **February 1865,** *Washington, D.C.*

AL.c1865.2A

Photograph by Lewis Emory Walker

Journalist Ben Perley Poore's description of Lincoln refers to the President's short hair. As in this portrait, possibly from February 1865, Lincoln's hair was cut short in preparation for sculptor Clark Mills's life mask, made that same month.

Mr. Lincoln used to wear at the White House in the morning, and after dinner, a long-skirted faded dressing-gown, belted around his waist, and slippers. His favorite attitude when listening—and he was a good listener—was to lean forward, and clasp his left knee with both hands, as if fondling it, and his face would then wear a sad and wearied look. But when the time came for him to give an opinion on what he had heard, or to tell a story, which something said "reminded him of," his face would lighten up with its homely, rugged smile, and he would run his fingers through his bristly black hair, which would stand out in every direction like that of an electric experiment doll.

March 4, 1865, *Washington, D.C.*

AL.1865.3B

Photograph by Alexander Gardner

On the day Lincoln delivered his Second Inaugural Address, John Wilkes Booth was in the crowd behind him. Washington's marshal, Ward Hill Lamon, later wrote about it.

Everybody knows what throngs assemble at the Capitol to witness the imposing ceremonies attending the inauguration of a President of the United States. It is amazing that any human being could have seriously entertained the thought of assassinating Mr. Lincoln in the presence of such a concourse of citizens. And yet there was such a man in the assemblage. He was there for the single purpose of murdering the illustrious leader who for the second time was about to assume the burden of the Presidency. That man was John Wilkes Booth. . . . Booth's plan was one of phenomenal audacity. So frenzied was the homicide that he determined to take the President's life at the inevitable sacrifice of his own; for nothing can be more certain than that the murder of Mr. Lincoln on that public occasion, in the presence of a vast concourse of admiring citizens, would have been instantly avenged. The infuriated populace would have torn the assassin to pieces, and this the desperate man doubtless knew.

March 6, 1865, *Washington, D.C.*

AL.1865.5A

Photograph by Henry F. Warren

The last photograph of Abraham Lincoln in life was taken at the White House by Massachusetts photographer Henry Warren. His friend Alexander Starbuck later told how it happened.

On the afternoon of the 6th of March, Mr. Warren sought a presentation to Mr. Lincoln, but found, after consulting with the guard, that an interview could be had on that day in only a somewhat irregular manner. . . . [He] was given to understand that the surest way to obtain an audience with the President was through the intercession of his little son "Tad." The latter was a great pet with the soldiers, and was constantly at their barracks, and soon made his appearance, mounted upon his pony. He and the pony were soon placed in position and photographed, after which Mr. Warren asked "Tad" to tell his father that a man had come all the way from Boston, and was particularly anxious to see him and obtain a sitting from him. "Tad" went to see his father, and word was soon returned that Mr. Lincoln would comply. In the meantime Mr. Warren had improvised a kind of studio upon the south balcony of the White House. Mr. Lincoln soon came out, and, saying but a very few words, took his seat as indicated. . . . At the time he appeared upon the balcony the wind was blowing freshly, as his disarranged hair indicates, and, as sunset was rapidly approaching, it was difficult to obtain a sharp picture.

April 24, 1865, *New York City*

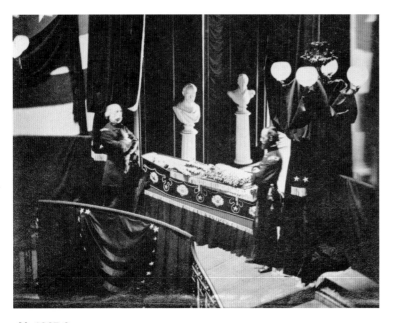

AL.1865.6

Photograph by Jeremiah Gurney, Jr.

After his death, Lincoln's face was photographed on one occa-sion, with the negatives confiscated by Secretary of War Edwin Stanton. A single saved print did not surface until 1952, when it was first published. Journalist David R. Locke—also known as Petroleum Nasby— was one of the hundreds of thousands to pay respects to the slain President.

I saw him, or what was mortal of him, on the mournful progress to his last resting-place, in his coffin. The face was the same as in life. Death had not changed the kindly countenance in any line. There was upon it the same sad look that it had worn always, though not so intensely sad as it had been in life. It was as if the spirit had come back to the poor clay, reshaped the wonderfully sweet face, and given it an expression of gladness. . . . The face had an expression of absolute content, of relief, at throwing off a burden such as few men have been called upon to bear—a burden which few men could have borne. I had seen the same expression on his living face only a few times, when, after a great calamity, he had come to a great victory. It was the look of a worn man suddenly relieved.

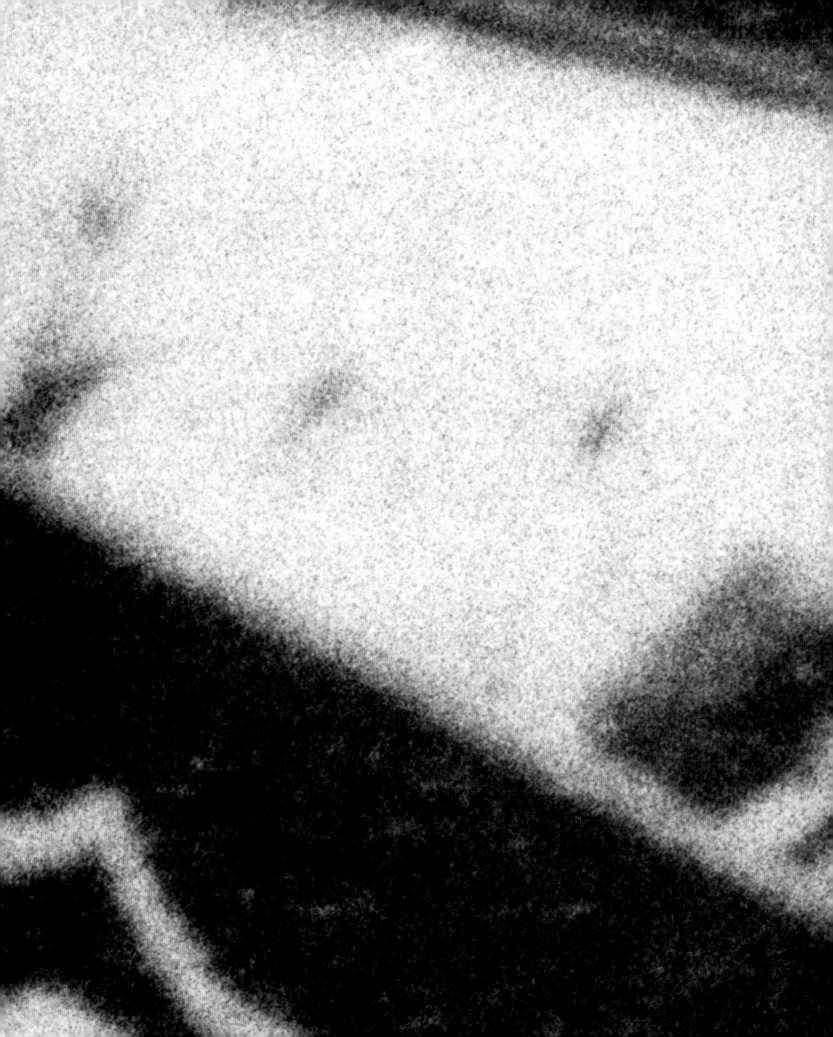

Additional Portraits

AL.1860.3C
Photograph probably by Preston Butler
Springfield, Illinois
May 20, 1860

AL.1860.3D
Photograph probably by Preston Butler
Springfield, Illinois
May 20, 1860

AL.1860.5D
Photograph by Alexander Hesler
Springfield, Illinois
June 3, 1860

AL.1860.13A
Photograph probably by Preston Butler
Springfield, Illinois
May 20, 1860

AL.1860.13B
Photograph by John Adams Whipple
Springfield, Illinois
Summer, 1860

AL.1860.15B
Photograph by Preston Butler
Springfield, Illinois
August 13, 1860

165

AL.1861.3B
Photograph by Frederick DeBourg Richards
Philadelphia, Pennsylvania
February 22, 1861

AL.1861.4B
Photograph by Alexander Gardner
Washington, D.C.
probably February 24, 1861

AL.1861.4D
Photograph by Alexander Gardner
Washington, D.C.
probably February 24, 1861

AL.1861.4E
Photograph by Alexander Gardner
Washington, D.C.
probably February 24, 1861

AL.1861.5
Unknown photographer
Washington, D.C.
March 4, 1861

AL.1861.6A
Photograph possibly by C. D. Fredericks,
James E. McClees, or W. L. German
Washington, D.C.
circa spring 1861

AL.1861.7B
Photograph by unknown operator for
Mathew B. Brady
Washington, D.C.
May 16, 1861

AL.1862.1A
Photograph by Alexander Gardner
Antietam, Maryland
October 3, 1862

AL.1862.1D
Photograph by Alexander Gardner
Antietam, Maryland
October 3, 1862

AL.1862.1F
Photograph by Alexander Gardner
Antietam, Maryland
October 3, 1862

AL.1863.1B
Photograph by Alexander Gardner
Washington, D.C.
August 9, 1863

AL.1863.1C
Photograph by Alexander Gardner
Washington, D.C.
August 9, 1863

AL.1863.1D
Photograph by Alexander Gardner
Washington, D.C.
August 9, 1863

AL.1863.2C
Photograph by Alexander Gardner
Washington, D.C.
November 8, 1863

AL.1864.1C
Photograph by Mathew B. Brady
Washington, D.C.
January 8, 1864

AL.c1864.3A
Photograph by unknown operator
for Wenderoth & Taylor
Washington, D.C.
circa 1864

AL.1864.4B
Photograph by Anthony Berger
Washington, D.C.
April 20, 1864

AL.1864.4C
Photograph by Anthony Berger
Washington, D.C.
April 20, 1864

AL.1864.5B
Photograph by Anthony Berger
Washington, D.C.
April 26, 1864

AL.1865.1B
Photograph by Alexander Gardner
Washington, D.C.
February 5, 1865

AL.1865.1C
Photograph by Alexander Gardner
Washington, D.C.
February 5, 1865

AL.c1865.2B
Photograph by Lewis Emory Walker
Washington, D.C.
circa February 1865

AL.1865.3A
Photograph by Alexander Gardner
Washington, D.C.
March 4, 1865

AL.1865.3C
Photograph by Alexander Gardner
Washington, D.C.
March 4, 1865

AL.1865.3D
Photograph by Alexander Gardner
Washington, D.C.
March 4, 1865

AL.1865.4
Photograph by William Morris Smith
Washington, D.C.
March 4, 1865

AL.1865.5B
Photograph by Henry F. Warren
Washington, D.C.
March 6, 1865

About the Portraits

This book reflects more than a century of collaboration. In the late nineteenth century, when Frederick Hill Meserve began collecting, preserving, and identifying the portraits of Abraham Lincoln, he found himself at the center of a growing circle of historians, journalists, teachers, collectors, artists, writers, and history buffs, all of whom had a passion for what had become known as Lincolniana. Looking back a century later, what is most remarkable was the trust that these people placed in one another. "There was no rivalry, we were all friends helping one another," Meserve explained. "I carried their want lists in my pocket and they handed over to me the photographs that came to them."

Meserve was not a photography collector by any modern definition. He was an image collector, whose goal was to be comprehensive. To this end he amassed a huge collection of original photographs, copies of originals, and copies of copies. As he pieced together the scattered puzzle pieces that made up the overall photographic record of Lincoln, he gave each image an M number to indicate its chronological place in the sequence. His system was to become the national standard.

In 1911 Meserve privately printed his first book, *The Photographs of Abraham Lincoln,* with 100 actual photographs mounted on handmade paper. Historian Carl Sandburg wrote, "[When] collectors of Lincolniana . . . got a Lincoln photograph they compared it with those in the Meserve book [and] gave it the Meserve serial number. And if they couldn't find it in Meserve, they sent him the original or a copy, saying, 'This looks like a new one,' and awaited the reply sure to come from Meserve."

Nearly a century later, the authors of this book worked with a panel of Lincoln scholars to bring Meserve's numbers up to date. The original M numbering system has been replaced with an AL numbering system, devised with the help of James Barber at the National Portrait Gallery. New research has required changes in Meserve's work and that of his successor Lloyd Ostendorf. Each AL number follows a pattern: it begins with the year the photograph was taken; is followed by a number to indicate the portrait session; and ends with a letter of the alphabet to differentiate poses at each session.

To make this book, the authors combed through Meserve's original prints, duplicates, copy images, modern prints, glass negatives, and modern negatives. We then combined these with images from James Mellon's set of Lincoln portraits. In the 1970s Mellon meticulously duplicated Lincoln photographs that he had collected, then

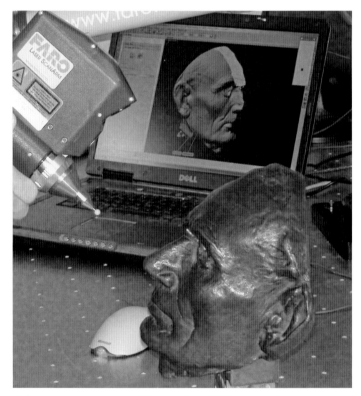

A laser scanner is used to create a 3-D image of Lincoln's 1860 life mask.

traveled the country photographing first- and second-generation Lincoln images wherever he could find them, to produce his highly praised book *The Face of Lincoln*. Because Meserve's work was so central to Mellon's project, he provided us with a full set of his images.

After compiling all the Meserve and Mellon prints, we selected what we determined were the three best versions of each image to bring to Chicago Albumen Works, a company that specializes in museum-quality digital reproduction. We asked experts there to select what they considered to be the best-quality source for each portrait and make high-quality black-and-white scans that would allow Lincoln's face to be enlarged with the greatest clarity. Since the original photographs varied in size, as did the face of Lincoln within them, these enlargements ran the gamut from relatively minor to quite extreme, leading to some startling results.

While this digitizing process was taking place, a second scanning project got under way to determine, as precisely as possible, the actual life measurements of Lincoln's head and face. An early bronze casting of the 1860 life mask by Leonard W. Volk was taken to Direct Dimensions, a 3-D imaging company, where the contours of Lincoln's face were captured and a two-dimensional grid was created.

Then in consultation with artist Clifford Ross and portrait sculptor Jim J. Nance at the Abraham Lincoln Art Gallery, we calculated a ten percent enlargement to the size of the life mask to compensate for shrinkage during the bronze casting process. The result is a face that is about 9½ inches from the chin to the crown of the head—not an overly large head for a man of Lincoln's size.

Head shots of Lincoln taken from different angles can be particularly difficult to size properly. By superimposing the corrected 3-D scans taken from the mask over these photographs, and tilting them appropriately along different axes, Elton Robinson, the designer of this book, was able to make the photographic enlargements come out as close as we can estimate to life-size.

And so the record of the face of Lincoln owes itself to hundreds of different individuals—to photographers, collectors, institutions, and scholars—and to a long tradition of study and publication. From this century-long collaboration, which reflects the work of so many people, emerges a candid, surprisingly modern look at Abraham Lincoln. It gives us yet a closer glimpse of the real man.

Different angles of the life mask are used to match the way Lincoln held his head in each of his photographs.

The life-size 3-D scans are superimposed over each portrait so that Lincoln's head can be accurately enlarged.

Text Sources

1846.1   *McClure's Magazine* 6, no. 1 (December 1895), p. 110.

1854.1   *Chicago Daily Journal*, October 30, 1854.

1857.1   Wayne Whipple, *The Story-Life of Lincoln* (Philadelphia, 1908), p. 335.

1857.2   Roy P. Basler, ed., *The Collected Works of Abraham Lincoln* (New Brunswick, N.J., 1953), 2:404.

1858.1   Ida Tarbell, *The Early Life of Abraham Lincoln* (New York, 1896), p. 113.

1858.2   Quoted in Lloyd Ostendorf, *Lincoln's Photographs: A Complete Album* (Dayton, Ohio, 1998), p. 14.

1858.3   *Collected Works*, 2:459.

1858.4   "Personal Recollections of Abraham Lincoln," *National Magazine*, February 1916, p. 841.

1858.5   Tarbell, *Early Life*, p. 215.

1858.6   *Collected Works*, 3:204–5.

1858.7   *Chicago Press and Tribune*, October 15, 1858, p. 2.

1858.8   Allen Thorndike Rice, ed., *Reminiscences of Abraham Lincoln by Distinguished Men of His Time* (New York, 1889), pp. 440ff.

1858.9   Tarbell, *Early Life*, p. 81.

1859.1   Moncure, Daniel Conway, *Autobiography, Memories and Experiences*, vol. 1, p. 317.

1859.2   *Collected Works*, 3:511.

1859.3   *Collected Works*, 3:512.

1860.1   Rufus Rockwell Wilson, *Intimate Memories of Lincoln* (Elmira, N.Y., 1945), p. 250.

1860.2   *Collected Works*, 4:48.

1860.3   *Century Magazine*, October 1882, p. 852.

1860.4   *Independent*, September 1, 1864.

1860.5A Rufus Rockwell Wilson, *Lincoln in Portraiture* (New York, 1935), pp. 89ff.

1860.5B *Collected Works*, 4:69f.

1860.5C Ibid., 4:68.

1860.6   Ibid., 4:60f.

1860.7   Ibid., 4:34.

1860.8   Ibid., 4:82.

1860.9   Whipple, *Story-Life*, pp. 336–7.

1860.10 Instructions to John G. Nicolay, [July 1860], Abraham Lincoln Papers at the Library of Congress.

1860.11 F. H. Pratt to Abraham Lincoln, July 7, 1860, Abraham Lincoln Papers at the Library of Congress.

1860.12 *Collected Works*, 4:111.

1860.14 *Collected Works*, 4:92.

1860.15A Rice, *Reminiscences*, p. 479.

1860.16 *Collected Works*, 4:129.

1861.1   Ibid., 4:160.

1861.2A "Analysis of the Character of Abraham Lincoln," *Abraham Lincoln Quarterly*, September 1941, p. 369.

1861.2B *Collected Works*, 4:190.

1861.3A Ibid., 4:240.

1861.4A Rice, *Reminiscences*, pp. 37ff.

1861.4C Michael Burlingame, ed., *With Lincoln in the White House* (Carbondale, Ill., 2000), p. 28f.

1861.6B Joshua Fry Speed, *Reminiscences of Abraham Lincoln and Notes on a Visit to California* (Louisville, Ky., 1884), p. 34.

1861.7A *Collected Works*, 4:341f.

1861.7C William Howard Russell, *My Diary North and South* (London, 1863), 37f.

1861.7D *Collected Works*, 4:385f.

1861.7E Ibid., 4:438.

1861.7F Charles Godfrey Leland, *Abraham Lincoln and the Abolition of Slavery in the United States* (New York, 1879), p. 108.

1861.8   *Douglass' Monthly*, September 1861.

1862.1B Francis B. Carpenter, *Six Months at the White House with Abraham Lincoln* (New York, 1866), pp. 20ff.

1862.1C Charles M. Segal, ed., *Conversations with Lincoln* (New York, 1961), p. 210.

1862.1E *Collected Works*, 5:460f.

1863.1A Tyler Dennett, ed., *Lincoln and the Civil War in the Diaries of John Hay* (New York, 1939), p. 76.

1863.1E *The Liberator*, January 29, 1864.

1863.1F *Collected Works*, 6:371f.

1863.1G Ibid., 6:410.

1863.2A Burlingame, *With Lincoln*, p. 109.

1863.2B *Century Magazine* 47 (February 1894), p. 597.

1863.2C Quoted in Carl Schurz, *Abraham Lincoln: A Biographical Essay* (Boston, 1947), frontispiece.

1863.2D *Collected Works*, 6:538.

1863.2E Gary Wills, *Lincoln at Gettysburg* (New York, 1992), p. 29.

1863.3   Unidentified newspaper clipping in Mary Edwards Brown Scrapbook (MESB X77), Meserve-Kunhardt Foundation.

1863.4   *Collected Works*, 7:24

1864.1A Anonymous ("Joseph") to Abraham Lincoln, January 4, 1864, Abraham Lincoln Papers at the Library of Congress.

1864.1B *Collected Works*, 7:117.

1864.1D *Diary of Gideon Welles* (Boston, 1911), 1:506.

1864.1E Eva Young to Abraham Lincoln, January 9, 1864, Abraham Lincoln Papers at the Library of Congress.

1864.2A Carpenter, *Six Months*, p. 35f.

1864.2B Hattie L. Luckett to Abraham Lincoln, February 9, 1864, Abraham Lincoln Papers at the Library of Congress.

1864.2C James Penfield to Abraham Lincoln, February 13, 1864, Abraham Lincoln Papers at the Library of Congress.

1864.2D Smith Stimmel, *Personal Reminiscences of Abraham Lincoln* (1997), p. 38f.

1864.2E   Noah Brooks, *Washington in Lincoln's Time* (New York, 1896), p. 285.

1864.2F   *Collected Works*, 7:185.

1864.3B   Ibid., 7:512.

1864.4A   Michael Burlingame and John R. Turner Ettlinger, eds., *Inside Lincoln's White House: The Complete Civil War Diary of John Hay* (Carbondale, Ill., 1997), p. 194.

1864.5A   Carpenter, *Six Months*, p. 91f.

1864.5B   Isaac Arnold, *The Life of Abraham Lincoln* (Chicago, 1884), pp. 451ff.

1865.1A   Russell H. Conwell, "Personal Glimpses of Celebrated Men and Women," in Agnes Rush Burr, *Russell Conwell: The Work and the Man* (Philadelphia, 1905), p. 356.

1865.1D   Rice, *Reminiscences*, p. 585f.

1865.1E   Rice, *Reminiscences*, p. 249f.

1865.2A   Ibid., pp. 230f.

1865.3A   Ward Hill Lamon, *Recollections of Abraham Lincoln* (Chicago, 1895), p. 266ff.

1865.5A   *Century Magazine*, October 1882, p. 853.

1865.6   Rice, *Reminiscences*, p. 452f.

Selected Bibliography

Photographic Histories

Frassanito, William A. *Gettysburg: A Journey in Time.* New York, 1974.

———. *Antietam: The Photographic Legacy of America's Bloodiest Day.* New York, 1978.

Holzer, Harold, Gabor S. Boritt, and Mark Neely, Jr. *The Lincoln Image.* Carbondale, Ill., 2005 (originally published 1984).

———. *Changing the Lincoln Image.* Fort Wayne, Ind., 1985.

Katz, Mark. *Witness to an Era.* New York, 1990.

Kunhardt, Dorothy Meserve, and Philip B. Kunhardt, Jr. *Twenty Days.* New York, 1965.

———. *Mathew Brady and His World.* Alexandria, Va., 1977.

Kunhardt, Philip B., Jr., Philip B. Kunhardt III, and Peter W. Kunhardt. *Lincoln: An Illustrated Biography.* New York, 1992.

Kunhardt, Philip B., III, Peter W. Kunhardt, and Peter W. Kunhardt, Jr. *Looking for Lincoln: The Making of an American Icon.* New York, 2008.

Lorant, Stefan. *Lincoln: His Life in Photographs.* New York, 1941.

———. *Lincoln: A Picture Story of His Life.* New York, 1952.

Mellon, James, ed. *The Face of Lincoln.* New York, 1979.

Meserve, Frederick Hill, and Carl Sandburg. *The Photographs of Abraham Lincoln.* New York, 1944.

Miller, Francis Trevelyan. *Portrait Life of Lincoln.* Springfield, Mass., 1910.

Neely, Mark, Jr., and Harold Holzer. *The Lincoln Family Album.* New York, 1990.

Ostendorf, Lloyd. *Lincoln's Photographs: A Complete Album.* Dayton, Ohio, 1998.

Ostendorf, Lloyd, and Charles Hamilton. *Lincoln in Photographs, an Album of Every Known Pose.* Norman, Okla., 1963.

Panzer, Mary. *Mathew Brady and the Image of History.* Washington, D.C., 1997.

Steers, Edward, Jr. *Lincoln: A Pictorial History*, 1983.

Tarbell, Ida M. *The Early Life of Abraham Lincoln.* New York, 1896.

Trachtenberg, Alan. *Reading America's Photographs: Images as History, Mathew Brady to Walker Evans*, New York, 1989.

Wilson, Rufus Rockwell. *Lincoln in Portraiture.* New York, 1935.

General Bibliography

Arnold, Isaac. *The Life of Abraham Lincoln.* Chicago, 1884.

Basler, Roy P., ed. *The Collected Works of Abraham Lincoln.* Vols. 1–8. New Brunswick, N.J., 1953.

Brooks, Noah, *Washington in Lincoln's Time.* New York, 1896.

Burlingame, Michael, ed. *With Lincoln in the White House.* Carbondale, Ill., 2000.

Burlingame, Michael, and John R. Turner Ettlinger, eds. *Inside Lincoln's White House: The Complete Civil War Diary of John Hay.* Carbondale, Ill., 1997.

Burr, Agnes Rush. *Russell Conwell: The Work and the Man.* Philadelphia, 1905.

Carpenter, Francis B. *Six Months at the White House with Abraham Lincoln.* New York, 1866.

Dennett, Tyler, ed. *Lincoln and the Civil War in the Diaries of John Hay.* New York, 1939.

Diary of Gideon Welles. Boston, 1911.

Lamon, Ward Hill. *Recollections of Abraham Lincoln.* Chicago, 1895.

Leland, Charles Godfrey. *Abraham Lincoln and the Abolition of Slavery in the United States.* New York, 1879.

Rice, Allen Thorndike, ed. *Reminiscences of Abraham Lincoln.* 8th ed. New York, 1889.

Russell, William Howard. *My Diary North and South.* London, 1863.

Schurz, Carl. *Abraham Lincoln: A Biographical Essay.* Boston, 1947.

Segal, Charles M., ed. *Conversations with Lincoln.* New York, 1961.

Speed, Joshua Fry. *Reminiscences of Abraham Lincoln and Notes on a Visit to California.* Louisville, Ky., 1884.

Stimmel, Smith. *Personal Reminiscences of Abraham Lincoln.* 1997.

Whipple, Wayne. *The Story-Life of Lincoln.* Philadelphia, 1908.

Wills, Gary. *Lincoln at Gettysburg.* New York, 1992.

Wilson, Douglas L., and Rodney Davis. *Herndon's Informants.* Carbondale, Ill., 1998.

Wilson, Rufus Rockwell. *Lincoln Among His Friends.* Caldwell, N.J., 1942.

———. *Intimate Memories of Lincoln.* Elmira, N.Y., 1945.

Acknowledgments

The authors thank the many people who helped make this book possible, starting with Esther Newberg, our literary agent and longtime friend, who first recognized the power of looking at Lincoln life-size. Thank you, Esther and Kari Stuart.

We thank the wonderful team at Alfred A. Knopf, whose president and editor in chief, Sonny Mehta, supported this book long before we delivered him an earlier one, *Looking for Lincoln*. We thank him for that trust. We also thank our editor, Andrew Miller, who helped shape this book, giving us encouragement, thoughtful ideas, and always the benefit of his good taste. And we give thanks to Sara Sherbill, who works at Andrew's side and from start to finish was enormously helpful. We thank Andy Hughes for overseeing the production of this book; Andy is the best in the business and we are very fortunate to work with him. We feel this way as well about the entire team at Knopf who worked on this project, including production manager Lisa Montebello, copy chief Lydia Buechler, copy editor Janet Biehl, designer Peter Andersen, and managing editor Kathy Hourigan. And once again we thank Paul Bogaards and Kim Thornton for overseeing publicity for the book. They are a pleasure to work with.

For the design of the book we turned to our longtime friend and collaborator, Elton Robinson. His simple, elegant hand and eye led to what you see on these pages. Thank you, Elton. And we thank the inimitable Chip Kidd for designing the book jacket. We also give thanks to our friends at Chicago Albumen Works, especially Doug Munson and Oleg Baburin, for their patient work creating extraordinary digital scans. And we thank Todd Kamelhar, Brian Dentel, and Mario Testani at Gelfand, Rennert and Feldman for keeping us on track along the way.

We say a special thank-you to Harold Holzer for writing the foreword to this book. A preeminent authority on Lincoln iconography, he is an accomplished author on the subject of Lincoln's life and memory, and serves as co-chair of the U.S. Abraham Lincoln Bicentennial Commission. Early on we also got his help when we developed a new numbering system for the Lincoln photographs. Harold, along with James Barber of the National Portrait Gallery, Tom Schwartz of the Abraham Lincoln Presidential Library and Museum, and Dan Weinberg of the Abraham Lincoln Book Shop, were all incredibly helpful.

At Kunhardt-McGee Productions we are grateful to Dyllan McGee, Mary Farley, Amy Rockefeller, Mike Maron, Jill Cowan, Tom Denison, Diana Revson, and Robert Gold for the constant help and encouragement they gave on behalf of the project. And we thank the trustees of the Meserve-Kunhardt Foundation: Laura Brown, Nina Freedman, Curt Viebranz, Dan Tishman, and Gene Young.

Most of all we thank our families. Margie and Suzy Kunhardt have given us their love and constant support. We thank them for putting up with our long hours. And we thank our children: Jessie, Philip, Harry, Clinton, Abby, Teddy, and George (the last three of whom are siblings of Peter Jr.). We gratefully acknowledge our revered forebears who bequeathed to us their knowledge and interest in Abraham Lincoln: Frederick Hill Meserve, Dorothy Meserve Kunhardt, and Philip B. Kunhardt, Jr. And lastly we thank our most avid supporter—Katharine Trowbridge Kunhardt—who is adored by us all and to whom we dedicate this book.

A Note About the Authors

Philip B. Kunhardt III is a writer and producer and is
currently a Bard Center Fellow. Peter W. Kunhardt is
executive producer of Kunhardt-McGee Productions.
Peter W. Kunhardt, Jr., is assistant director of the
Meserve-Kunhardt Foundation. They are the authors
of *Looking for Lincoln*, and along with their father, the
late Philip B. Kunhardt, Jr., Philip and Peter are authors
of *Lincoln: An Illustrated Biography*. The Kunhardts
are based in Westchester County, New York.

A Note on the Type

The text of this book was set in Century Expanded, designed early in the 1900s by Linn Boyd Benton (1844–1932) to update the original Century, cut in 1894 by his father, Morris Fuller Benton (1872–1948), in response to a request by Theodore Low De Vinne for an attractive, easy-to-read typeface to fit the narrow columns of his *Century Magazine*. The younger Benton, working for his father's American Type Founders Company, also created such other popular variations of Century as Century Old Style and Century Schoolbook.

Book design by Elton Robinson